a gift to

_____

from

_____

date

_____

Comfort for Mothers of Miscarried Babies

A Time to be Borne

Compiled by
Dianna Overholt
and Sue Hooley

Carlisle Press
WALNUT CREEK

ISBN: 1-890050-94-6

Any reference in this book to miscarried babies as angels is figurative, and
is not meant to infer that they become one of God's celestial beings.

Cover and text design: Teresa Hochstetler
Printing: Carlisle Printing

Carlisle Press
WALNUT CREEK
2673 TR 421
Sugarcreek, OH 44681

Dedication

This little volume is dedicated with love to those whose caring lifted us in our *time to be borne.*

Acknowledgments

We are grateful to these women for blessing us with insight and encouragement by their written words.

Bechtel, Annette (Mrs. Nolan)	Estacada, OR
Beachy, Mary Ellen (Mrs. Mark)	Dundee, OH
Birky, Jewel (Mrs. Gerald)	Halsey, OR
Brubaker, Paula (Mrs. Kervin)	Elizabethtown, PA
Eash, Char (Mrs. Mel)	Topeka, IN
DelValle, Lillian (Mrs. Dave)	Halsey, OR
Martin, Danette (Mrs. Ken)	Waterloo, ON, Canada
Miller, Marcia (Mrs. David)	Seymour, MO
Miller, Marilyn (Mrs. Mark)	Seymour, MO
Miller, Rosey (Mrs. Harold)	Uniontown, OH
Smucker, Laura (Mrs. John)	Minsk Mazowieck, Poland
Troyer, Ivy (Mrs. Jerry)	Wasilla, AK
Weaver, Jo Ellen (Mrs. John)	Conrath, WI

To every thing there is a season,
and a time to every purpose under the heaven:
A time to be born, and a time to die;
a time to plant, and a time to pluck up that which is planted;
A time to kill, and a time to heal;
a time to break down, and a time to build up;
A time to weep, and a time to laugh;
a time to mourn, and a time to dance;
A time to cast away stones,
and a time to gather stones together;
a time to embrace, and a time to refrain from embracing;
A time to get, and a time to lose;
a time to keep, and a time to cast away;
A time to rend, and a time to sew;
a time to keep silence, and a time to speak.

—Ecclesiastes 3:1–7

Introduction

Sue: In Ecclesiastes 3, King Solomon describes my experiences in the past four years. I thought that having a baby meant *a time to be born.* But when my pregnancy ended by miscarrying, *a time to die,* it was the beginning of a new season in my life.

I like to be organized and plan ahead so I had mentally started a to-do-before-baby-comes list. *Who should I ask to help me? How should I decorate the nursery?* The next few months looked full and exciting. My primary focus was on the new little somebody. But my future was suddenly rearranged as I found myself forced into the *time to mourn* stage.

Surprised at the emotions and thoughts that assailed me, it was my *time to weep.* It was a sad and lonely time for me. No one else had loved or prayed for this little life like I had. So it seemed that no one grieved his passing like I did.

I was in the *time to heal* stage when Dianna and I became acquainted. Dianna had just joined a Writer's Workshop by Mail group that I was in (WWM IV) when I mentioned the idea of compiling a miscarriage book. I had previously helped compile *The Hand that Rocks the Cradle,* a book for new mothers.

Dianna: Because I hadn't yet miscarried, I didn't give Sue's idea much thought. But a month later when I found myself in her shoes, I really wished for a book like that. I wanted to read how other ladies felt. I wanted someone to tell me how to react! I'm so thankful for the Bible because it contained answers to all the questions I asked. As I searched its pages, jotting down what the Lord showed me, the vision for a miscarriage book grew.

Sue: Six months later, Dianna got in touch with me. I hadn't given up the idea of a book, but I didn't seem to have clear direction from the Lord. When she contacted me, I wondered if this was my answer. Well, it was! Our *time to heal* turned into *a time to speak,* amazingly across the 1,800 miles between us. It was also a *time to* *blend.* Is that one in Ecclesiastes? Our personalities are opposite (she loves unfamiliar words, I prefer the common) but I think God loves blending differences to bring about His plans!

Dianna: I'm glad Sue knew what a big project we were undertaking. I didn't! I think that the phrase *a time to gather stones together* paints an accurate picture of our endeavor. The Israelites gathered stones to make a memorial whenever they wanted to mark a certain incident in their journey. In a way, this book is a memorial made by fifteen of us to mark the place in our lives where God carried us. Stone by stone the book slowly took shape, and we hope that the resulting memorial will show itself an altar of worship to our readers.

Sue: We had many who helped build the book to its completion. We especially thank those who reviewed the entire manuscript, and our writing groups, WWM IV and WWM VIII, for critiquing our submissions. The Lord never let us down in providing help and inspiration when we needed it!

Dianna and Sue: We want you, our readers, to discover what we did—that although a miscarriage is not *a time to be born,* it is *A Time to be Borne* by our heavenly Father. Whenever you are in your private journey of sorrow or uncertainty, may you reach the thrilling conclusion of Ecclesiastes 3:11, that "He hath made everything beautiful in his time."

The Seasons of the Soul

Laura Waldron

When you feel cast down and despondently sad,
And long to be happy and carefree and glad,
Do you ask yourself, as so often I do
Why must there be days that are cheerless and blue?
Why is the song hushed in the heart that was gay?
And then I ask God, "What makes life this way?"

And His explanation makes everything clear;
The soul has its seasons, the same as the year.
Man, too, must pass through life's autumn of death
And have the heart frozen by winter's cold breath.
But spring always comes with new life and birth,
Followed by summer to warm the soft earth.

Oh, what a comfort to know there are reasons,
Why souls, like nature, must have their seasons.
Bounteous seasons and barren ones, too—
Times for rejoicing and times to be blue.
For with nothing but sameness, how dull we would be,
Only life's challenges set the soul free,
And it takes both a mixture of bitter and sweet
To season our life and make it complete.

More Than Enough

Danette Martin

"He that spared not his own Son, but delivered him up for us all, how shall he not with him freely give us all things?" —Romans 8:32

It's inevitable; you'll lose this pregnancy." The doctor's voice was kind but his words were like a leaden bell tolling a death knell.

My outward calm belied my inward yelling, "But this baby's alive! His growth swells my tummy; already I feel his timid nudges and tiny kicks."

"The baby is living," the doctor's words marched on. "But the sac of waters is already dropping. Reversing the progress would only invite infection. Your options are induction or allowing nature's course. It could be a few hours or a few days."

In the van, tears streamed down my cheeks as I groaned inaudibly, "Home to wait until our baby's birth. I mean his death. All this from an incompetent cervix. I hate it!" My mute ranting continued, "I know lots of other moms have miscarried. This far along, too. But haven't their babies died in utero? My baby's perfectly healthy; his house is just too weak to hold him in. Poor little one—he's forced out too early. My living baby! Born to die! Does anyone understand this agony? It is too much for me."

> *How calmly may we commit ourselves to the hands of Him who bears up the world.* —Richter

Out of the screaming silence came a sweet, soothing voice. "I know. I released my sinless Son from a perfect, most secure environment into an evil world, to death. Love motivated Me; victory was My goal. I had you in mind."

Peace melted my cold cynicism. Ah, yes, Someone does understand. So infinitely, my pain is dissolved in the reality.

It is enough, more than enough. ✑

Safely Home

Dianna Overholt

"In a moment… we shall be changed."

—I Corinthians 15:52

So what kind of drugs have you been taking? Marijuana? Cocaine?" The E.R. nurse's brisk voice floats from across the hallway into our room.

Good, I'll welcome any sort of distraction right now. Anything to lift me from this hole of suspense. It is midnight, but my husband and I cannot leave the hospital until we find out the reason for my bleeding. Is my pregnancy over?

I don't even have to strain to hear the nurse.

"So you overdosed and decided to come here," she says. "Our records show that this is the second time you are admitting yourself. Who brought you? A friend? I'm showing here that your parents kicked you out of home."

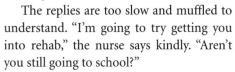

The replies are too slow and muffled to understand. "I'm going to try getting you into rehab," the nurse says kindly. "Aren't you still going to school?"

A young man. On drugs. No home… *Your parents kicked you out of home.*

Is his mother this very night longing for the time when she had rocked him to sleep?

Some mother's baby has rejected her love. Some mother's baby has crushed the dreams of what he could become. A mother has lost her baby.

Footsteps in the doorway. The results from the ultrasound are here. They show that our baby's life is gone.

I look at the ceiling, tears sliding down my face. *Gone, but safely at home in Your arms, Jesus.* ⮌

How beautiful heaven must be. —A.S. Bridgewater

Good-bye, Little One

Dianna Overholt

Angel baby—
You're not staying,
Though we're praying…
     Praying…
          Praying.
Must you leave us?
Must you really
     Go away, away, awaying?

Angel baby—
     Wait! I'm saying—
     Haven't yet begun conveying
          That your life would be a joy!
          And oh, are you a girl or boy?
Please, delay…
          delay…
               delaying.

Angel baby,
     Scarcely weighing,
     Like a butterfly a'playing
          Feels the sunshine,
          Flutters upward,
Leaves the graying…graying…graying.

Tiny cherub,
     Light arraying,
     Can you hear what Mommy's saying?
          Mommy's longing…
          Mommy loves you.
Go, wee one,
          With Jesus staying.

Good-bye, Little Angel.

Humble As This Little Child

Annette Bechtel

**"Whosoever therefore shall humble
himself as this little child, the same is greatest
in the kingdom of heaven."** —Matthew 18:4

My husband and I gazed lovingly at the still form of our first son. I had been only in the 17th week of my pregnancy, and our perfectly formed, but incredibly tiny son had been born far too early for any chance of survival.

Grief washed over me in a flood and I longed for a hundred what-might-have-beens. Wasn't God being too hasty in plucking our baby bud? *We would have loved him, Lord…*

Our daughters came into the room to see Joey, the brother they would never play with or get upset at for meddling in their girlish affairs. They stared at his doll-like features and reached out to stroke his fragile skin.

"I'm not sad," four-year-old Nolita declared. "Jesus will make the baby well."

"Yeah," two-year-old Joelle agreed. "We can share the baby with Jesus. That will be nice."

They didn't realize it, but their words brought great healing to the fresh, gaping wound in my heart. I needed to hear those simple words of acceptance, to check my attitude toward the One who works all things for good.

I gratefully drew our precious daughters into my aching, empty arms and found sweet peace in leaning on the everlasting arms of my heavenly Father. ✎

---

*Keep a journal of your feelings and prayers.
You'll be able to chart your progress.*

Empty Arms

Laura Smucker

**"Cast thy burden upon the Lord,
and he shall sustain thee."** —Psalm 55:22a

All night I hear the lusty cry of a newborn in the next hospital room. A mother has just given birth to her dream and delight, her baby. After long months of waiting, her arms are enfolding a precious new life, created in heaven just for them. And here I lie—feeling as if a chunk of myself has been ripped away. Empty, everything is empty. The room, my arms, my heart…

Our loss wasn't just any baby; it was a gift straight from God. I had a growing love for this tiny life, an excitement about adding another one to our family of five. But now I will go home with empty arms. "Why God?" I cry. "For this child I prayed." But He has not granted my petition, and I feel like a weeping Hannah in a lonely temple.

God, I want to accept this as Your plan for my life. I have always prayed, "Thy will be done." I still believe that even though my heart feels broken. Minister comfort to my heart so that I can sense another's loss. Although I may, like Hannah, have a woman next door who is bursting with happiness, You can give me grace to rejoice with her.

There is something better than understanding God, and that is trusting Him.

Lord, help me to see Your goodness even in suffering, Your grace even through pain, and Your joy in sorrow. Grant me peace.

The Gift of Blood

Danette Martin

**"For the wages of sin is death;
but the gift of God is eternal life through
Jesus Christ our Lord."** —Romans 6:23

I felt so... gray. Not only had I lost our baby the previous day; I had also lost a good deal of blood. My world had shrunk to the size of my corner hospital room, and a hazy world at that.

My thoughts blurred like my vision. *I'm glad the awful game of wait, dread, wait, dread is over... that nurse has a motherly touch... but, oh, I feel ghastly... Mrs. Chesney hemorrhaged to death (in this day and age!)... will I die?*

Several hours and two units of blood later, I lie resting, pondering the amazing transformation I was experiencing. My skin stopped tingling, my vision cleared, and my thoughts took on more structure.

Life's colors seemed brighter, more intense. The universe expanded beyond the hospital walls.

Gratitude trickled out of a me-focused heart. My perking up had cost someone time, effort, and a tiny measure of life one day at a blood donor clinic. The grateful trickle widened to a stream. I wished I could tell that person what his gift meant to me.

Then the spiritual parallel gripped me: "And you hath he quickened, who were dead in trespasses and sins" (Ephesians 2:1). That was I. Cold and gray in sin-death. Brought back to life by His blood. Amazing Love! It cost Jesus His very life one day at Calvary.

The stream of thanks surged into a soul-flood: "Lord, Your Gift means everything to me!"

Thank God for sending His precious Son to die for your sins.

It Isn't an "It"

Jewel Birky

"Before I formed thee in the belly I knew thee; and before thou camest forth out of the womb I sanctified thee, and I ordained thee a prophet unto the nations." —Jeremiah 1:5

Losing my baby after nine short weeks of pregnancy brought with it a sudden confusion. Unprepared for what had just taken place, my shocked mind kept asking, *What happens to an unfinished baby?* I had never given it any thought before. I knew that when a newborn baby died, its soul went to be with Jesus. I knew that abortion is sin because it is killing a human life. I knew that my baby had been once living and growing, and now it was dead. But how could all this indescribable matter that had come out of me in the last hours be my baby, whose soul had gone to heaven?

Oh, I wanted to believe it! I tried picturing it in heaven. But what was it? I didn't know if it was a boy or a girl. I'm not even sure that I saw when I miscarried it. It wasn't formed yet; was it just an "it"? How could I be assured that even an unformed child was still recognized by God?

Think of ten glorious things your baby is experiencing in heaven.

God gave me a clear answer through Psalm 139.

"My substance was not hid from thee, when I was made in secret," David says. *God knew him as a person from the moment he was conceived.* "In thy book all my members were written… when as yet there was none of them." *God knew who David would become before his own mother even knew she was carrying him!* "In continuance [they] were fashioned, when as yet there was none of them." *God will not leave any of His work incomplete. He finishes what He begins.*

My baby is not a nameless, unfinished child! We never named our baby, but God did. "The Lord hath called me from the womb; from the bowels of my mother hath he made mention of my name" (Isaiah 49:1b). It isn't an "it", but a perfect sinless soul in the presence of God. What sweet comfort God brought to me through His Word.

Surely a great part of heaven is the many innocent souls of babies whom the Father loves with infinite tenderness. ◅

Peace

Dianna Overholt

**"I will both lay me down in peace,
and sleep: for thou, Lord, only makest
me dwell in safety."** —Psalm 4:8

Usually the visits with my OB-GYN are fairly routine. She asks how I'm feeling, says "Show me your baby!" and then we listen to the heartbeat.

But today—two days after my miscarriage—I am in her office and I want to be anywhere but here. There's no druma-druma-druma of a heartbeat. Instead, she confirms that my hormone levels are falling rapidly and that my miscarriage is complete.

Oh no, it's not complete. It is only beginning, I think bitterly as we head home. I read during the rest of the day—a book, a magazine, a newspaper; filling my mind's emptiness so I don't have to think.

"Get a story," I tell my four-year-old at bedtime as I hunker under the covers with a can of cheese curls for his snack.

He returns, clutching his favorite book about a chameleon lizard. He spies the cheese curls as he snuggles in and a wide grin lights up his face. He laughs out loud.

"I'm just *so* happy!" he exclaims.

A book… cheese curls…and a warm mommy to cuddle up to. Wouldn't it be nice if my happiness came this simply?

Am I supposed to be happy right now? What will it take to make me happy? The psalmist said, "Happy is the man that hath his quiver full of [children]!" And I've just had an arrow taken away.

I don't think God expects me to have a bubbling-over feeling of joy at the moment. But He does want me to be at peace. "O… greatly beloved, fear not: peace be unto thee, be strong, yea, be strong. And when he had spoken unto me, I was strengthened, and said, Let my lord speak; for thou hast strengthened me" (Daniel 10:19).

God can give me an inner peace, a peace that comes when I, through faith, commit myself and this situation to Him. "And the work of righteousness shall be peace; and the effect of righteousness quietness and assurance for ever. And my people shall dwell in a peaceable habitation, and in sure dwellings, and in quiet resting places" (Isaiah 32:17-18).

"Joy cometh in the morning," King David said. Until then, I can rest in the peace that my God does all things well. ⤙

Peace is beautiful. —Whitman

And the peace of God, which passeth all understanding, shall keep your hearts and minds through Christ Jesus.

Finally, brethren, whatsoever things are true, whatsoever things are honest, whatsoever things are just, whatsoever things are pure, whatsoever things are lovely, whatsoever things are of good report; if there be any virtue, and if there be any praise, think on these things.

Those things, which ye have both learned, and received, and heard, and seen in me, do: and the God of peace shall be with you.

But I rejoiced in the Lord greatly, that now at the last your care of me hath flourished again; wherein ye were also careful, but ye lacked opportunity.

Not that I speak in respect of want: for I have learned, in whatsoever state I am, therewith to be content.

I know both how to be abased, and I know how to abound: every where and in all things I am instructed both to be full and to be hungry, both to abound and to suffer need.

I can do all things through Christ which strengtheneth me.

Philippians 4:7–13

Is It a Secret?

Jo Ellen Weaver

**"They shall bear the burden… with thee,
that thou bear it not thyself alone."** —Numbers 11:17b

I won't tell, I thought to myself. *No one knows about it, so why should I tell?*

It seemed like the logical thing to do. Since it was only Monday, I had all week to recover from my miscarriage and no one would need to know.

Tuesday went okay but by Wednesday I wasn't so sure. I was so tired and so weepy. Lying on the couch was far easier than scrubbing the dishes that had been accumulating. The two preschoolers fended for themselves the best they could and I didn't care.

When my friend stopped in on her way home from town, I was embarrassed at the chaotic condition of our usually tidy house.

I jumped up from the couch and began running dishwater. I didn't want her to know! But my swollen eyes and disheveled hair were enough to make her ask, "Is something wrong? You look like you're not feeling well."

I burst into tears. Suddenly it didn't matter who knew. The whole story tumbled out. She gave me a hug and wept with me. "Go lie down and let me bring you a cup of tea," she said.

Before long she had the dishes washed, the kitchen swept, toys popped in their places, and was reading my toddlers a story. Her caring heart was a salve to my torn emotions. Her calm, assuring manner brought comfort to my confused children. The worried looks on their faces were replaced with happy little smiles.

She was only there for an hour, but by the time she left I wondered why I had wanted to keep it a secret. My burden was eased and the pain of my loss was not nearly as great when shared with a friend. ⌣

*Remember that the circumstances around you are never
as significant as whose arms are around you.*

You Never Know

Mary Ellen Beachy

"If the Lord will, we shall live, and do this, or that." —James 4:15b

50% *off all wallpaper in stock; Saturday only!* Sounded like a good deal to me. I wanted new wallpaper for the nursery. The floral paper with blue stripes had been there for years and was stained in places. I was sure I would have enough energy to repaper it long before August when our baby was due.

"It's fine with me if you go on Saturday," my husband said. "I'll stay here with the children." Shopping alone! What a treat!

On Friday I hurried with the usual laundry and cleaning. I was looking forward so much to Saturday. But at noon I caught my breath. I was spotting bright red blood.

When mild cramping began that evening, my heart cried out, *Oh, God, is this another miscarriage?* I was only two and a half months pregnant, and scared. My husband and I slept very fitfully that night. I could feel his love, care, and support surround me.

During the night our dreams for another baby (*a daughter would be nice, Lord!*), were borne away to heaven. Instead of going shopping the next morning, I lay flat in bed. As I looked at our six children, more precious than ever, I realized that having a healthy baby is a greater miracle than I will ever know.

Make it a priority to give a hug and a compliment to each of your children today.

We can dream about having more children, but only God can fulfill those dreams.

We can plan our days, weeks, and months, but it is God who orders our lives.

We can rest, because the outcome is held in His hands. ⌐

With God All Things Are Possible

Paula Brubaker

"The things which are impossible with men are possible with God." —Luke 18:27b

O ur friends were coming to visit and I couldn't wait! They were more than just mere friends; they felt like family. As couples, we dated over the same time and in the same home, were married within weeks of each other, and each of our first two children were born close together in age.

Their third child had just been born. Because of my previous miscarriages, their baby would be six months older than the one we were expecting. But I was just so thankful to have hopes again! I started sewing a little suit for her baby in anticipation of their visit.

But my hopes were not to be fulfilled. On the day they were coming, I realized that the life I was carrying had died and I would not be having the baby we had dreamed of.

I finished sewing the suit in tears. My thoughts tumbled, *I wonder if I'll be brave enough to hold her baby. No, no, I can't do it!* And yet, another part of me yearned for the comfort of holding the newborn and letting my tears fall on his tiny face.

Those were precious moments. My friend and I sat in the dim living room alone. She put a comforting arm around my shoulder as I snuggled the baby in my arms. His face was such a healthy pink, his cry so lusty and his little lips and nose so perfect. He was too wonderful for me. I spoke between my sobs, "It just doesn't seem possible that we'll ever have a completely-formed baby again."

The words she whispered were so simple but so consoling. "With God all things are possible."

There it was, a Bible verse; words fitly spoken! I couldn't doubt what she said—it was nothing less than biblical truth.

So this promise has stayed with me. Again and again it comes as a balm of comfort, a ray of hope. *With God all things are possible! Nothing is difficult for Him.* ❧

Look up five verses that have the word "hope" in them.

Share one of them with a friend or family member.

Then Job answered the Lord, and said,

I know that thou canst do every thing, and that no thought can be withholden from thee.

Who is he that hideth counsel without knowledge? therefore have I uttered that I understood not; things too wonderful for me, which I knew not.

Hear, I beseech thee, and I will speak: I will demand of thee, and declare thou unto me.

I have heard of thee by the hearing of the ear: but now mine eye seeth thee.

Job 42:1–5

God's Hands

Dianna Overholt

**"Behold, I have graven thee
upon the palms of my hands."** —Isaiah 49:16a

W e are in God's hands."
Have I heard you say these words recently? I automatically echo them myself, for they are comfort food for the soul.

But how did we get into His hands? Just what are God's hands like? How recently have you looked at them?

Start by examining His fingers. Use a telescope to look at the sky with its never-been-numbered stars, and we're glimpsing only a fraction of what those fingers have fashioned. Or soak up the rays of the estimated 27,000,000° F fiery sun. King David specifically says that these are the work of God's **fingers**. What about a smoking, spewing volcano? That's the **fingertip** touch of God on a mountain

(Psalm 104:32). It's no wonder that when God's **finger** touched Jacob's thigh, the sinew shrank, crippling his leg for life.

If God were holding us in His fingertips, it would be more than sufficient. But God's not content to put us there. He has placed us in His **hands** and no one is able to pluck us out! David realized that God would never let go of him when he asked, "Where can I hide from You? Even if I'd live in the uttermost parts of the sea—six miles underwater, Your **hand** would still lead me, and Your right **hand** would still hold me."

How did we get into His hands? It all comes back to the adjective that the Bible uses more than any other to describe the Lord's **arm**. It is *stretched-out.*

So say it again—we are in God's hands! Stretched-out, placed-under, and folded around. How secure we are! ꙮ

---

*There is no stay so strong as unreserved abandonment
of self into God's hands.* —Sidney Lear

Has God Forgotten Me?

Paula Brubaker

**"Be of good courage, and
he shall strengthen your heart."** —Psalm 31:24a

You don't… do you ever feel…" my concerned sister hesitated over the phone. "Does this make you bitter toward God? This is your third miscarriage in one year!"

I was so devastated over the events of the previous day that I hadn't really analyzed my feelings. The thirteen-week checkup had dashed our hopes to bits like broken glass. How could God have allowed us to be so deceived? Every day that we had thanked Him for another little one, He knew that life had already fled at seven weeks. And we had never sensed it at all.

"It makes me wonder what trick He is going to pull on us next," I answered, swiping at the tears rolling down my cheeks. Later, I couldn't believe I had said such distrusting words but that is exactly how I felt. At the moment, God was so hard to understand and I hardly knew how to pray. I felt as if I had been slapped in the face.

Have you also discovered that in the severe disappointments of life, God can suddenly seem very far away and you can feel utterly forsaken?

All that I have seen teaches me to trust the Creator for all that I have not seen. —Emerson

Rest assured that God will not and does not forget His own. One of Satan's favorite lies that he whispers to God's children is this: *Your God cannot be trusted. Your God has forsaken you.*

When I begin to feel like God has lost my file or forgotten my number, I turn again to Psalm 31:14-24. Yes, Lord, I trust in Thee. Thou art *my* God. My times are in Thy hand… Let the lying lips of Satan be put to silence, which speak grievous things… Oh, how great is Thy goodness, which Thou hast laid up for them that trust in Thee… I said in my haste, I am cut off from before Thine eyes…O love the Lord, all ye His saints. Be of good courage, and He shall strengthen your heart, all ye that hope in the Lord.

God will never forsake us! ✑

Jesus Loves the Mothers

Dianna Overholt

> "Thus saith the Lord; A voice was heard in Ramah, lamentation, and bitter weeping; Rahel weeping for her children refused to be comforted for her children, because they were not." —Jeremiah 31:15

I hadn't meant to study a verse like this one, especially not while I was recovering from a miscarriage!

Unsure of what I wanted to read, I paged through my Bible, thinking, *I need something about Jesus' love of children…some comforting word about Jesus wanting my child to be with Him.*

I started reading Jesus' life story in Matthew and it wasn't long before I found 2:16-18, "And [Herod] slew all the children that were in Bethlehem, and in all the coasts thereof, from two years old and under… Then was fulfilled that which was spoken by Jeremy the prophet saying, In Rama was there a voice heard…"

I wept for the mothers. I had to turn back to Jeremiah 31 and read the background surrounding the prophecy.

Know what I discovered? A different sort of comfort than what I was searching for. Instead of revealing God's love of children, he reaffirms God's love for mothers.

He speaks to several kinds of mothers: expectant mothers, mothers in labor, and mothers who have lost their children.

Listen to verse 9. "They shall come with weeping, and with supplications will I lead them: I will cause them to walk by the rivers of waters in a straight way, wherein they shall not stumble."

Verse 17: "And there is hope in thine end, saith the Lord, that thy children shall come again to their own border." (The hope of heaven!)

And in verse 25 He says, "For I have satiated the weary soul, and I have replenished every sorrowful soul."

Yes, Jesus loves the little children of the world.
Jesus loves my child.
Jesus loves the mothers of the world.
And He loves me. ☞

Jesus Loves Me

Jesus loves me! this I know,
For the Bible tells me so;
Little ones to Him belong;
They are weak but He is strong.

Yes, Jesus loves me;
Yes, Jesus loves me;
Yes, Jesus loves me;
The Bible tells me so.

Jesus loves me! He who died,
Heaven's gate to open wide;
He will wash away my sin,
Let His little child come in.

Yes, Jesus loves me;
Yes, Jesus loves me;
Yes, Jesus loves me;
The Bible tells me so.

God's Thunderings

Danette Martin

"Thou wilt keep him in perfect peace, whose mind is stayed on thee: because he trusteth in thee." —Isaiah 26:3

"Mom, I don't like thunder-rain," confided our four-year-old after he was tucked into bed one damp night.

"But I don't hear any thunder and it's not even raining right now," I responded. The little lad didn't say anything and I could tell his brain was busy.

Then, "Mom, why does it thunder?" he questioned.

I replied, "Because God wants us to hear His voice."

"But why does it thunder so often?"

"I think God wants us to know for sure that it's His voice."

"He wouldn't have to thunder so much. After one time I know it's Him."

"We don't need to be afraid of thunder," I assured my son, "because we know whose voice it is. When we are not afraid, that's called 'trust.'"

"That's right, Mom. Trust, because we like Him so much."

Our conversation ended but my thoughts went on. Thunder-rain. My own life has been full of it. Five deaths in our family in the past year and a half. *God, I don't like thunder-rain either.* I feel like telling God He's thundered once too often.

The words of assurance I gave to our son came back to me: "We don't need to be afraid of the thunder because we know whose voice it is."

I make a commitment. "God, these thunderings are really scary. But I know they are Your voice. So I will go on in trust. Because I love You so much."

He did not say, "You shall not be tempest-tossed, you shall not be work-weary, you shall not be discomforted." But He said, "You shall not be overcome." —Julian of Norwich

---

Letter to God

Ivy Troyer

**"Weeping may endure for a night,
but joy cometh in the morning."** —Psalm 30:5b

Lord, when You allowed that little life to begin several months ago, only You knew that a little one was there. We hoped that life had begun, we were certain that life was there, but You knew. And You cared.

While attending brother Mark's wedding, visiting in Guatemala, fulfilling my daily household responsibilities, and planting the tiny flower seeds, that little life was growing. Who was that life to become, and what tasks would he accomplish by and by?

Lord, Your plans were higher than ours. Only You knew that soon You would take this little life back to Yourself.

While You were forming this little one so carefully, You made the eyes, not to see earth's fading beauties for a time, but to see only Jesus' face and the eternal glories of heaven. The tiny feet and toes were never intended to walk on our grass and wade through mud puddles. They were intended only for heaven's floor. The small fingers never had a chance to grasp at no-nos. They know only the touch of Jesus' hand. The ears have never heard earth's clamor, only heaven's joy. The little voice needs never ask, "Mama, where does God live?" because that voice is praising God in His presence. And that soul was never given to us to guide since it is already "safe in the arms of Jesus."

Spend a few minutes outside after dark, listening to the night sounds.

Lord, the grief is not only in what was, but for what might have been. Then I remember the beauty and perfection of what *is,* and I am comforted in knowing that You do all things well from beginning to end.

(Lord, what name did you give our baby?) ⤳

Questions

Mary Ellen Beachy

"Though he slay me, yet will I trust in him." —Job 13:15a

"Why, Mama, why?"

Two-year-old Micah is at my elbow as I use my mother-in-law's serger sewing machine. "Why is that thing sticking up, Mama? What are you sewing? Why do you use that machine, Mama, why?"

Giving my inquisitive son an answer only invites more questions! They pop up like jack-in-the-boxes.

"What are fat humps, Mama? What is fur?" he says from my lap as I read him a Bible story.

Or he sees me getting some pills out of a bottle. "What is that, Mama? Is it for you, or for you?"

Today I am as full of questions as my little son.

Why, God, why? Have I had four miscarriages because I am not

learning the lessons You want me to learn? If I am not to keep a baby, why do I conceive? If I miscarry because there is something abnormal with the fetus, why do some people keep their "'special" babies?

I know that God is trying to teach me something and my first response is to ask more questions. Does He mind my questioning?

I don't really mind my son's many questions. I bask in his love and trust.

God is calling me to do the same. To bask in His love. To trust when things make no sense at all. Job did that. His trials were much more severe and dramatic than mine, yet he said, "Though he slay me, yet will I trust in him."

So what shall I do with my questions?

Give them to me, my Saviour says. *Child, lay your weary head on My breast. Love Me more, trust Me fully. Find in Me your all in all.*

He is the answer. ✎

Be creatively grateful. Then you'll always have something to celebrate. —H. Jackson Brown, Jr., 2002

Going for Gold

Danette Martin

**"But he knoweth the way that I take:
when he hath tried me,
I shall come forth as gold."** —Job 23:10

Y ou were beautiful before, but God must want you even more beautiful. I know you'll come out of this trial as gold." Tears sent tremors through my twin sister's voice in her phone call to me from a neighboring country.

Gold? I silently repeated. *Who wants to go for gold? If heading for gold clears one stack of sympathy cards off the coffee table just to receive a fresh batch, if it renders my heart a growing cavern of ache, if it makes me feel adrift and anchorless on a rough sea at midnight, count me out. I'll settle for plain tin.* Focusing only on the heat of my hardship made me lose sight of the pure and priceless end result.

Gold. God is going after gold! He knows that fire removes the dross of pride, deceit, and complacency in me. He reminds me that the more often metal enters the fire, the more durable and valuable it becomes. The Refiner desires a weight of gold so shining He can view a reflection of His own beauty in it.

Oh, God, let me catch a glimpse of Your anticipation as You turn up the heat on the refining furnace.

> *Adversity is the mint in which God stamps upon us His image and superscription.*
>
> —Henry Ward Beecher

Does God Need a Reason?

Jo Ellen Weaver

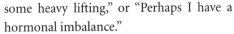

> "Then I beheld all the work of God, that a man cannot
> find out the work that is done under the sun:
> because though a man labour to seek it out, yet he shall
> not find it; yea farther; though a wise man think to know it,
> yet shall he not be able to find it." —Ecclesiastes 8:17

What was the cause of your miscarriage?" someone bluntly asked.

Even though my aching heart rebelled at being asked again, I replied, "God does all things well. Evidently He thought we needed this experience more than we needed a baby."

I could have said something like, "I varnished a bureau," or "I did

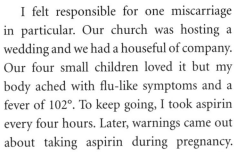

some heavy lifting," or "Perhaps I have a hormonal imbalance."

I felt responsible for one miscarriage in particular. Our church was hosting a wedding and we had a houseful of company. Our four small children loved it but my body ached with flu-like symptoms and a fever of 102°. To keep going, I took aspirin every four hours. Later, warnings came out about taking aspirin during pregnancy. I immediately connected it to my miscarrying two weeks after the wedding. Of course I felt guilty.

But in dealing with that guilt I found peace in reading the words of the wisest man who lived. "I applied mine heart to know, and to search, and to seek out wisdom, and the reason of things..." he said. "Then I beheld all the work of God, that a man cannot find out the work that is done under the sun: because though a man labour to seek it out, yet he shall not find it."

To guiltily grope for reasons is pointless when even Solomon declared that we cannot understand the work of God. We can take precautions to ensure a safe pregnancy, but sometimes we aren't even aware of the pregnancy, or the danger of our actions. Ultimately it is what God wills. "For all this I considered in my heart… that the righteous, and the wise, and their works, are in the hand of God," Solomon concluded.

Does God need a reason? No, but my reasoning needs God. ॐ

Perhaps the reason that God doesn't always give us the answer to the whys of our existence is that He knows we haven't got the capacity to understand the answer. In learning to depend on God, we must accept that we may not know all the answers, but we know who knows the answers. —Max Lucado

Walking With the Savior, © copyright 1993 by Max Lucado. Used by permission.

Trusting Our Father

Anonymous

"I will trust, and not be afraid:
for the Lord Jehovah is my strength and my song;
he also is become my salvation." —Isaiah 12:2b

My little girls asked their father for permission to go with their friends on a special outing. This time Daddy denied their request. Although he had a good reason, it was wisest not to explain.

My girls were heartbroken. They couldn't understand. They deduced that Daddy was "mean". Life was so unfair!

I watched them, and wished they would just trust their father. He was always so good and generous with them. Why didn't they focus on all the times he had played with them, brought them fun presents, and called them sweet names? Didn't they realize that Daddy knew best?

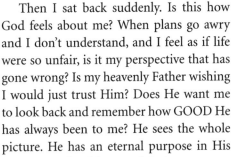

Then I sat back suddenly. Is this how God feels about me? When plans go awry and I don't understand, and I feel as if life were so unfair, is it my perspective that has gone wrong? Is my heavenly Father wishing I would just trust Him? Does He want me to look back and remember how GOOD He has always been to me? He sees the whole picture. He has an eternal purpose in His wise decisions, although He may not be able to explain it to me.

Dear Father, let me trust You completely!

Create a home environment that is a glimpse of heaven.

—H. Jackson Brown, Jr., 2002

Overwhelmed

Laura Smucker

**"From the end of the earth will I cry unto thee,
when my heart is overwhelmed: lead me to the rock
that is higher than I."** —Psalm 61:2

My heart is breaking.
Everything around me reminds me of my loss…
People don't understand that this feels like a death;
They don't know how to respond.
They say it was God's mercy and love…
Maybe there was something wrong.
It was nature's way of selecting a healthy fetus…
Who knows, it might have had handicaps.
They mean well…
But it was my baby,
Not just fetal tissue.
I carried it under my heart for two months
And I will grieve silently if I have to
Over the loss of never knowing this little one.
I will grieve when no one around me knows it…
When I see a baby buggy on the street;
When I see mothers cuddling pink and blue bundles;
When I see my sweet little clothes all packed away;
When I see the empty cradle.
Yes, I will grieve.
I must.
It is the only path to healing.

God is beginning to mend my heart…
He is ministering to my brokenness.
I can rest under His wings…
He will take my hand
And lead me through this dark valley of sorrow.

The Choice to Rejoice

Jewel Birky

**"Rejoice with them that do rejoice,
and weep with them that weep."** —Romans 12:15

I'm with a friend who lives several hours away. We don't see each other very often and so we have much to visit about. She tells me how sorry she is to hear about my miscarriage, and she gives her ear to my sadness. It feels good to confide in a friend and feel her sympathy.

But she is pregnant. The conversation moves on, and she begins talking about her pregnancy and the coming baby. A deep hurt goes through my heart as I hear her talk. Our babies were due around the same time. The longing to still be carrying my baby is almost overwhelming. How can she be so uncaring as to talk like this in my presence?

But wait! I am being very unfair. She sorrowed with me in my loss; shouldn't I be willing to rejoice with her in her joy? And so I do. It hurts intensely, but I also feel a surprising sense of healing. Truly it is God's way to rejoice with those that rejoice and to weep with those that weep.

Help me, dear Lord, to sincerely rejoice with those who are expecting little ones, and fill this void in my life that was made when my own baby went to be with You. Amen. ⤺

Send a care package to someone who is battling cancer.

Acceptance and Pardon

Anonymous

**"For my thoughts are not your thoughts,
neither are your ways my ways, saith the Lord."** —Isaiah 55:8

Horror grasped my heart as I discovered that I was threatening to miscarry. Baby number six hadn't been an easy pregnancy. Almost every night our nine-month-old tossed with intermittent sleep. She missed nursing. Her inflamed gums told the tale of little teeth that struggled to appear. I was exhausted *all* the time and hadn't welcomed another pregnancy.

But the last week had gone better and acceptance was much easier.

I certainly wasn't ready for this. "O God," I cried, "please let me keep this little one, if it be Your will, and forgive me for being so slow to accept it."

God heard my prayer, but He chose to take our little unknown baby home to be with Him. I wept bitter tears. I agonized about my attitude. Feeling so small because I had shared my feelings with others, I dreaded going to church.

*Take a ten-minute stroll.
It will refresh your spirit.*

Sunday morning as I looked at the pale reflection in the mirror my eyes swam in tears. What a contrast it was to the bright-eyed, rosy-cheeked girl of long ago. The duties of motherhood made me look older than my 29 years.

I walked away from the mirror and picked up the mirror of God's Word. Opening to Isaiah 55:8, I read, "For my thoughts are not your thoughts, neither are your ways my ways, saith the Lord." Then my eyes lit on the preceding verse, "Let the wicked forsake his way, and the unrighteous man his thoughts: and let him return unto the Lord, and he will have mercy upon him; and to our God, for he will abundantly pardon."

I whispered in the stillness of the hour, "Your way is best. I will accept it. Thank you for the abundant pardoning through your Son."

I went to worship with the other believers with a peace that was mine once again as I yielded to His plan. ◄

Reasons

Dianna Overholt

"As for God, his way is perfect."

—II Samuel 22:31a

It is 7:00 a.m. and my special friend, Francie, is sharing the first coffee of the day with me. She wraps her hands around her mug and stares for a moment at the cream swirled in it. Then she looks shyly at me and smiles. "I don't know if I should say this," she begins. "It might be too hard for you."

"Oh, no, Francie, go ahead," I assure her.

"Dianna, you are very special to me. I know I can say this." She smiles again and gets serious. "I want you to know that you are very special to God and I pray for you. I was praying in my prayer closet and I told the Lord, 'Lord, Dianna and Michael went to the hospital to have a baby and they didn't bring a baby home. Why, Lord? Why?

I know they are in much pain and sorrow.' And I was praying and praying for you and do you know what Jesus told me? He said, 'Francie, I love Dianna and I will take care of her. Dianna and Michael will have another baby.' I am so glad to hear Jesus say that and I want to tell you about it."

I wish you could meet Francie.

In my imagination, when God made Francie He said, "I'll add an extra chromosome to this little girl to make her very special." He had a definite reason for giving Francie Down's Syndrome. Twenty-eight years later, it is easy to see why Francie is with us, dispensing hugs, love, and earnest prayers.

I wish it would be easy to see God's reason for my miscarriage. As God was forming my child did He say, "Grow within your mommy for a few months and then come back to Me"? Did He think that I needed this experience more than I needed a baby? Was this the reason?

My baby lives in heaven. *God has a reason.* Francie has come close to death several times. But she's here today. *God has a reason.*

I love Francie for telling me of her prayers. But at this point I'm not allowing myself to think much about another pregnancy. What comforts me at the moment is that *God has a reason for everything!*

It is now 7:30 a.m. and Francie and I are sharing our second cups of coffee. Francie doesn't talk as she watches the steam curling up from her cup.

But her life speaks of sovereign reasons. ⌇

Invite a friend for tea.

For thou art my lamp, O Lord: and the Lord will lighten my darkness.

For by thee I have run through a troop: by my God have I leaped over a wall.

As for God, his way is perfect; the word of the Lord is tried: he is a buckler to all them that trust in him.

II Samuel 22:29–31

Are You Coming Apart?

Dianna Overholt

**"And God opened her eyes,
and she saw a well of water."** —Genesis 21:19a

So you are coming apart, you say?
I'm glad to hear that. Coming apart is the best thing that can happen to you!

No, I don't mean *falling apart*. Going to pieces only makes a puzzle hard to reconstruct. Please don't fall apart. *Come apart.*

These are Jesus' words. Read this advice to His weary disciples in Mark 6:31, "Come ye yourselves apart into a desert place, and rest a while."

Chances are, you already feel as if you are in a personal Sahara. But to rest? Is there rest in a desolate, deserted habitat?

First of all, realize that you are not in a wasteland. It may be dry,

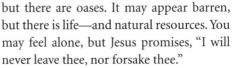

but there are oases. It may appear barren, but there is life—and natural resources. You may feel alone, but Jesus promises, "I will never leave thee, nor forsake thee."

Of all the people with nomadic experience, it is the Israelites that can teach us a most vital lesson. Do you remember how they grieved the Lord? *They limited the Holy One in the desert.*

They were never left without God's presence in the wilderness. Never once did they have to forage for food. God was there. He provided. But they complained and doubted, ultimately restricting themselves from the best that God could have given them. What made them so faithless? Didn't they see the pillar of fire? Or was their sight set on the shifting sand dunes?

The sand, the wind, and the barrenness will try to distract you from the hidden life that is really there. Let them be a background that only shows up more beautifully the cloud of light, the Elims, the manna that you discover.

It may be a desert. But when you come apart with Jesus, it can be *rest.*

Come Apart and Rest

Words and Music by Doreen R. Berry

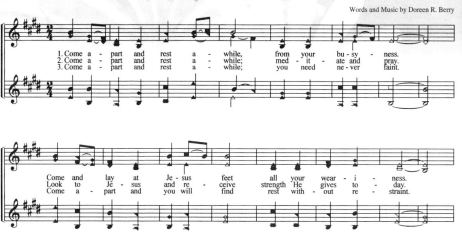

1. Come a - part and rest a - while, from your bu - sy - ness.
2. Come a - part and rest a - while; med - it - ate and pray.
3. Come a - part and rest a - while; you need nev - er faint.

Come and lay at Je - sus feet all your wear - i - ness.
Look to Je - sus and re - ceive strength He gives to - day.
Come a - part and you will find rest with - out re - straint.

Leave your hur - ried thoughts be - hind; peace and qui - et - ness you'll find.
Lin - ger here with long - ing soul; you'll find zeal to reach the goal;
Here find cour - age, here find love, life and hope from heav'n a - bove;

As you seek the Fath - er's best, Come a - part and rest.
Con - fi - dence to meet each test. Come a - part and rest.
Here is where your soul is blest. Come a - part and rest.

How beautiful it is to do nothing, and then rest afterward.

—Spanish Proverb

The Healing Habit

Lillian DelValle

**"Who forgiveth all thine iniquities;
who healeth all thy diseases."** —Psalm 103:3

Have you lost three, four, or more babies through miscarriage? If so, then you can probably understand how I felt as I listened to my doctor.

"It has happened again," he said curtly. "You are likely what we call a habitual aborter."

You don't know how your words cut my heart into little pieces! I wanted to scream. I already knew that something was wrong with my body. This was my second miscarriage. But an aborter! What a stinging word.

I tried natural remedies, and doctoral treatment, and prayed for a miracle. Even though I lost six more, I could never call myself "an aborter of babies." "Miscarrying" was much more gentle. But the reality of either one was cruel.

I struggled with worthlessness. *I'm no good; I can't even give my husband a baby!* I battled bitterness. *Lord, You know how much we want a baby to hold!* My negative thoughts became habitual, creating a chain of bitterness that went on and on in my mind until it affected me physically.

Through my physical illness, God opened my eyes. He seemed to say, "Child, you have carried this load alone for too long. You have not turned to Me. Aren't you weary of traveling this road of bitterness?"

The chain of bitterness was broken as I poured out my heart and begged for His forgiveness.

I am thankful that I had a God of "habit" to see me through. Although I frequently miscarried, often wept, and struggled with bitterness, He was the constant that remained. Because of His very character, His unchangeable habit, He never failed me. Over and over again I received peace as I submitted my all to Him, bringing healing both spiritually and physically. ✎

Ask a child to name five things for which he is thankful.

Miscarriage Zone— Handle with Prayer

Sue Hooley

"Casting all your care upon him, for he careth for you." —1 Peter 5:7

At least you still have a baby to cuddle," consoled my friend. *Yes, but he looks like a giant compared to the new one we were anticipating.*

"Just think, your baby is in heaven and sometime you can have another one," another friend encouraged. *I know, but I wanted this one.*

"You probably became pregnant too soon after your latest miscarriage and that is why you miscarried again," said yet another friend. *No way*, I wanted to shout, *the doctor said they were totally unrelated.*

Sometimes I wished that I could drape a blaze-orange sign around my neck that said, "Miscarriage Zone— Handle with Care!"

I berated myself for being so touchy. I knew that my accusations were unfair. I was expecting my friends to understand how I felt, even when they had not experienced the same thing. Phone calls, a bouquet of flowers, scrumptious cookies and other acts of kindness were reminders that my friends truly cared about me.

Wait in prayer. Call on God and spread the case before Him. Express your unstaggering confidence in Him. Wait in faith, for unfaithful, untrusting waiting is but an insult to the Lord. Wait in quiet patience, not murmuring because you are under affliction, but blessing God for it. —Spurgeon

God invites us to cast our care upon Him. If you feel a little misunderstood, talk to your heavenly Father. He knows exactly how you feel and He loves you. You will feel comforted when the miscarriage zone is handled with prayer.

Emptying My Tearcup

Laura Smucker

"My tears have been my meat day and night." —Psalm 42:3a

Does anyone care that I am grieving after losing the baby I carried for only two short months? I long to burrow in my cocoon of grief and wrap in its strands of self-pity.

But the Lord says, "No, not yet." Shortly after I return from the hospital, my sister gives birth to a baby girl. What a bittersweet day! My heart rejoices with her as tears stream down my cheeks. My cup is brimful of sorrow.

Can I think about myself now? The Lord says, "No, you need others in your life to help you through your grief." On the way home from the hospital, my husband and I stop at the airport and pick up three young men visiting our mission in Poland. For the next two weeks, visitors surround us.

When will I have time to steep in my loneliness? I think frantically. Tears plop and sink into my steaming cup of tea. I feel physically

weak and emotionally shattered. Life hasn't been easy with all the extra faces around. But I find healing as I open my guest book. "Thank you for opening your home to me, especially in the middle of a painful experience," one entry reads. Even our guests care about what is happening.

Now that they are gone I can think about my heartache. But the answer is "No" again. A friend drops by for tea. My cup of sadness is swallowed up in her story as she unburdens her heart, sharing many things from her past. My heart begins to heal as I share in her struggles. She needs me to help her find the way to God. She needs a friend to show her love and acceptance. She has many questions. I must find Scripture verses to help her.

God brings me daily opportunities to pour myself into the lives of my husband, my children, and my friends. As I fill their cups to overflowing with love and joy, my cup begins to empty of my grief and loneliness. ⌒

A little Consideration, a little Thought for Others, makes all the difference. —Eeyore, by A.A. Milne

---

Can Grief Be Measured?

Anonymous

"But my God shall supply all your need according to his riches in glory by Christ Jesus." —Philippians 4:19

I shook my head, blinked, and readjusted the closely-written page in my hand. Surely I had misread it. But no, there in neat, precise, black ink handwriting were the well-meaning words of a friend: *"You know, Susan had a miscarriage at 18 weeks, and to me, that's a lot worse than losing one at 14 weeks, as you did…"*

After recovering from a surprise attack of indignation, I actually smiled at the humor of it. Of course it was worse, even though the difference in our losses was that of mere weeks. Every week, even every day longer of pregnancy made a miscarriage worse. My own overactive imagination could easily conjure much more tragic situations: a sister's stillborn child; a friend losing a baby only hours after his birth; the tragic accident that claimed a toddler. I knew well enough that our loss was a small one compared to the things others have faced and survived.

Have patience and endure; this unhappiness will one day be beneficial. —Ovid

But a loss it was, nevertheless, and to us, a very significant one. Can grief be measured? Even though we were very aware of others suffering far worse things, we still had to grieve.

Grief is totally irrational. What makes perfect sense to you might be sheer nonsense to another. Don't belittle it. Face it. Take time to grieve. Sorrow. Cry. Talk to God about it, alone or with your husband; but don't wallow in self-pity. And don't harbor bitterness. Do something for somebody else. Pray for someone who is suffering. Try to find something to smile at once in a while. And when somebody says something that seems tactless to you, try to take it as the encouragement or comfort it was meant to be, remembering that those same words may well be healing ointment to another.

"My God shall supply all your need according to his riches in glory by Christ Jesus," also includes meeting the needs of our tattered emotions, or the roller coaster of our thoughts during this time. God understands grief. After all, didn't He give up His only Son?

Where Are They?

Jo Ellen Weaver

When a dear friend lost a baby in her first trimester, I tried offering the same comfort that I had received after miscarrying for the second time in a year. "Now you have at least one of your children safely home," I said.

She quickly informed me that she didn't believe that miscarried babies go to heaven. "No? Really—I—" My thinly-scarred wound broke open from the piercing pain of the recent past.

I couldn't say anything. But I had to know the truth for the sake of my comfort. I had to know for the sake of those I would seek to console in the future. "Please, give me an answer," I demanded of my husband. "Not an opinion, but a true biblical answer. When does eternity begin? At conception, at 4½ months into pregnancy, at 7 months, or not until 9 months? Does it only begin if a baby takes its first breath? Why is abortion wrong if my little babies will not have an eternity?"

We searched the Scriptures and this is what we found:

Isaiah 49:1b: "The Lord hath called me from the womb; from the bowels of my mother hath he made mention of my name."

Jeremiah 1:5: "Before I formed thee in the belly I knew thee; and before thou camest forth out of the womb I sanctified thee, and I ordained thee a prophet unto the nations."

Psalm 139:13-16: "For thou hast possessed my reins: thou hast covered me in my mother's womb. I will praise thee; for I am fearfully and wonderfully made: marvellous are thy works; and that my soul knoweth right well. My substance was not hid from thee, when I was made in secret, and curiously wrought in the lowest parts of the earth. Thine eyes did see my substance, yet being unperfect; and in thy book all my members were written, which in continuance were fashioned, when as yet there was none of them."

Oh, what a comfort to know exactly where our three precious babies are! Yours is there, too, safely home in the presence of our Maker, forever! ✎

Pray for your pastor and his wife.

To My Baby

Sue Hooley

I loved you from the start,
but God loved you even more.

I was eager for the first doctor appointment
so I could hear the "thump thump" of your little heart,
but those little drumbeats were silenced
before I ever heard them.

Already, I dreamed of fluffy blankets and
tiny clothes to make you warm and comfy,
but now you are experiencing total comfort.

I looked forward to hearing your first healthy cry;
instead, the angels heard the first noises
your tiny lungs ever made.

I anticipated the moment when your siblings
would walk into the hospital with big, expectant eyes
to take their first looks at you.
But then, you received a heavenly welcome
when you joined your little cousins.

I looked forward to cuddling you and
smelling your sweetness. But instead,
Jesus' caresses are oh, so gentle.

I thought of the joys you would bring and
I was so excited. I just couldn't wait.
But God had other plans and they couldn't wait.

Little one, I know you so little, but love you so much.
You never experienced pain or sin. You didn't even know about
heaven. But now you are there, in a place that Mommy can only
imagine. I miss you. But how can I wish you back?

Stepping Through Sorrow

Char Eash

"Trust in him at all times; ye people, pour out your heart before him: God is a refuge for us. Selah." —Psalm 62:8

Are you having one of those days when you'd love to draw the drapes and crawl back under the covers? (Perhaps you're thinking that it would keep your hormones from bouncing off the wall!) It's easier to drift into reverse than to deliberately take action over our feelings and emotions.

But God is a God of progression, not digression. "Move forward to the things that are before," He says. He's not even asking us to take giant strides. Baby steps in the right direction will still move us forward. Here are some simple steps that can keep us going:

1. Every morning, thank God for life and one other blessing you are grateful for. Even though you don't *feel* thankful, decide you *will* be.

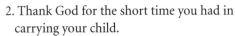

2. Thank God for the short time you had in carrying your child.
3. Remind yourself that God is in control and makes no mistakes.
4. Share your feelings openly with your husband. Don't assume that he knows how you feel, or that you know how he feels. Accept where he is at in his emotions.
5. Name him/her. Mention the child by name, not just "the baby."
6. Acknowledge to God at least one "blessing" you can see from the loss of this child. (Difficult, but it's a *giant* step forward!)
7. Tell Jesus just how you feel. Imagine yourself sitting on His lap and crying out to Him. Ask Jesus to give you a personal verse from His Word.

"Yea, though I *walk* through the valley of the shadow of death, I will fear no evil: *for thou art with me*"(Psalm 23:4). The best part about moving ahead is that we are not alone. ✎

Allow yourself ten minutes for a good cry.
Set the timer, get alone, and pour out your heart before God.
When the buzzer sounds, dry your tears, surrender your
circumstances to the Lord, and move on.

The Lord is my shepherd; I shall not want.

He maketh me to lie down in green pastures: he leadeth me beside the still waters.

He restoreth my soul: he leadeth me in the paths of righteousness for his name's sake.

Yea, though I walk through the valley of the shadow of death, I will fear no evil: for thou art with me; thy rod and thy staff they comfort me.

Thou preparest a table before me in the presence of mine enemies: thou anointest my head with oil; my cup runneth over.

Surely goodness and mercy shall follow me all the days of my life: and I will dwell in the house of the Lord for ever.

Psalm 23

Room to Run

Dianna Overholt

"I will be glad and rejoice in thy mercy: for thou hast considered my trouble; thou hast known my soul in adversities; and hast not shut me up into the hand of the enemy: thou hast set my feet in a large room." —Psalm 31:7-8

L ord,
   You have been merciful to me. You are considering my trouble. How well you know my soul!

But I hadn't seen clearly until now that You have set my feet in a large room.

I have felt all along as if I were in a room. My miscarriage happened, and I cannot get out of the circumstances. They box me in, forcing me to look at their walls.

I could let myself think that I am in a prison. But Lord, you have not shut me up into the hand of the enemy. For it is a large room.

How does my daughter act when I set her feet down in a large room? She runs and runs and runs. Sometimes in circles, sometimes in zigzags, but she never seems to tire of running.

You have wisely chosen this room for me. Will I beat on the walls or will I use this room for spiritual exercise?

The first thing I must do is quit focusing on the walls and look upward into Your merciful face. Only as I do this will I then be able to move my feet… to *run and not be weary, to walk and not faint.*

No weariness nor fainting? Lord, take my hand! ✐

One's outlook is part of his virtue. —Alcott

A Friend's Healing Touch

Dianna Overholt

"A friend loveth at all times." —Proverbs 17:17a

Today is my husband's birthday. My friend and I are staring at a jagged half of his birthday cake. The other half is still stuck in the Bundt® pan.

"Everything around here is either broken or dying!" I wail as we gape at the ruins. "This morning one of our tiger fish was floating belly-up in our aquarium. Then while I was lying in bed, all I could see through the window was brown grass, dying gladiolas, Edward's deflated swimming pool, and some of his broken toys."

As if to confirm it, the dishwasher knob falls off in my friend's hand a minute later.

She is here because of my miscarriage a few days earlier. She brings cinnamon rolls, and tidies up my kitchen and gathers our trash to take with her.

As she leaves, she gives me a hug. "I love you," she says.

She may not know it, but right now her friendship and caring are part of the glue that's keeping me from disintegrating like the broken things around me. At the same time that God has taken something precious from me, He's been reaffirming His love through my friends.

> *Christ moves among the pots and pans.*
> —Teresa of Avila

Touches of my friends are everywhere—a trio of roses in a baby bootie vase, a cloth-lined basket of homemade cookies, fresh fruit, a stack of clean pans from all the meals brought in. Have I been this caring to others?

I read Mark 2:1-5 and realize as never before how our friends play a role in our healing. The man with the palsy was "borne of four." They uncovered the roof, let down the bed, and when Jesus "saw *their* faith, he said unto the sick of the palsy, Son, thy sins be forgiven thee."

I feel a kinship with the palsied man. My friends are bearing me to Jesus through prayer and tangible acts of healing.

But I don't want to stay on the stretcher for long. I am ready to take my turn in bearing up my friends, even if it's something as small as caring about a cake that flops. ✑

A Time to Talk

Jewel Birky

"Confess your faults one to another, and pray one for another, that ye may be healed. The effectual fervent prayer of a righteous man availeth much." —James 5:16

D o people have to find out that I had a miscarriage? I don't want to tell anyone except our families and my best friend," I told my mom after we lost our baby.

I can't understand now what caused me to react that way. I'm normally a talkative person but my first response to our loss was to clam up. Maybe I was afraid of obligatory pity or of hearing someone say the wrong thing to me. Perhaps I thought that I would heal faster if I could just be treated normally by my friends.

But soon I realized that by hiding my hurt, I was keeping others  from helping me and praying for me. The Scripture says, "Confess your faults *(or could we say sorrows?)* one to another, and pray one for another, that ye may be healed. The effectual fervent prayer of a righteous man availeth much" (James 5:16).

I learned to talk about it and healing came through sharing the hurt. Friends sent cards, letters, and a beautiful scrapbook. They prayed for me in my time of grief.

Now that my talkativeness has returned, I have to be careful not to overdo it. What is my purpose for sharing my story? Is it to show what I can endure or is it to praise the One who gave me the strength to handle it? Is it to show that I have faced a greater pain than some others may have, or is it to tell what God has taught me through this loss? Is it to make others know how sad I am, or is it to plead for their prayers?

We need the wisdom of God to know when to share our feelings with others, and when to go to Him alone and pour out our hearts.

I want to share with others to receive their help and prayers. I want to bear the burden with those who are suffering the same grief that I have experienced. I want to leave all else to God and rest in His healing power at work in my life, for in the final analysis it is He alone who is the source of our healing and strength. ∽

The true way to soften one's troubles is to solace those of others. —Maintenon

Two are better than one; because they have a good reward for their labour.

For if they fall, the one will lift up his fellow: but woe to him that is alone when he falleth; for he hath not another to help him up.

Again, if two lie together, then they have heat: but how can one be warm alone?

And if one prevail against him, two shall withstand him; and a threefold cord is not quickly broken.

Ecclesiastes 4:9–12

From Grieving to Giving

Annette Bechtel

"But to do good and to communicate forget not: for with such sacrifices God is well pleased." —Hebrews 13:16

I looked at the word again. Grieving. Was "giving" really hidden in it? Yes! Removing the *r* and *e* left the word "giving" in plain sight.

Changing grieving to giving is a simple procedure on paper. But is it easy in real life? When I'm dealing with the pain of loss, when I'm reeling in the epicenter of a huge disappointment, when I'm just plain depressed, can I let go of a ME-focus to reach out to others?

I know a first-time mother whose baby was stillborn. In her sleepless early-morning hours, she sat at her sewing machine, fashioning doll clothes for nieces and dresses for her friends' babies.

A young man dying with AIDS took time to write an encouraging card to my mom during her battle with lung cancer.

The lives of these present-day saints reveal character I long to exemplify. I want to taste the joy that results from sharing during sorrow.

To turn my grieving into giving, I must remove dominating "*M-E*" from my line of vision and focus afresh on the supreme giver, Jesus. He looked far beyond the grief of the cross and gave His entire life for me. ✎

Give what you have. To someone it may be better than you dare to think. —Longfellow

---

A New Approach

Sue Hooley

**"If any of you lack wisdom, let him ask of God,
that giveth to all men liberally, and upbraideth not;
and it shall be given him."** —James 1:5

Through a crack in the bathroom door, I watched in fascination as my three-year-old son began his favorite job of brushing teeth. Determinedly he sque-e-e-zed the tube, but his chubby hands just weren't strong enough. The previous user had left the cap off, and the toothpaste had dried up around the opening. My son pondered this challenge for only a moment, then he put the tube on the floor. Stomp! The sought-after toothpaste spurted onto the linoleum. He scooped up the paste with his toothbrush and continued on with his usual routine.

Sometimes we, too, need to check our reactions to problems. Are you encountering dead-end responses? Perhaps you need a new approach. Instead of giving the naughty toddler another spanking, give him "mommy time" with a story and a snack. If you are frustrated that your husband does not automatically know how you feel, maybe you need to just kindly tell him. Instead of a deep sigh and rolled eyeballs, try a smile and a joke when you wipe up spilled milk.

> *Post James 3:17 on your refrigerator. Ask God daily for this kind of wisdom.*

Sometimes a new approach can help us work through grief. Instead of crying yourself to sleep every night, curl up with a cup of tea and meditate on the Word. If the days seem long and lonely, find a friend that needs your help.

If we ask God for wisdom, He will give it liberally. The best approach to any problem is to first approach the throne of grace.

God Loves You

Jewel Birky

"Yea, I have loved thee with an everlasting love: therefore with lovingkindness have I drawn thee." —Jeremiah 31:3b

*D*id God take my baby because He knew I wouldn't be a good mother?

Maybe He thinks I've made too many mistakes in my Christian life.

I didn't want a baby right away after we were married, so He may have taken this one to punish me.

Have these kinds of thoughts plagued you, too? We wonder, "Why me?" Is God trying to tell us something?

You can be sure that He's not saying the horrid things in the above paragraphs. Because God isn't like that. If God gave us exactly what we deserved, punishing us for every mistake and failure, we would

be miserable indeed! God does not want us to feel guilty for physical circumstances beyond our control.

Whatever happens in our lives, God always has something for us to learn. Try not to wonder why it happened but ask God for grace to accept that it happened.

What are some of the valuable lessons I learned from my miscarriage? I learned that God is in control of my life, and His ways are best. I learned to think of heaven as a nearer, more real place than I had before. I was drawn closer to my husband as we shared the first real sorrow of our married life. I learned that God will heal hearts that are hurting if we let Him. I learned how to sorrow with others who face the same experiences.

Most of all, I learned how much God loves me. God loves you, too, with an everlasting love. ꙮ

There are some things you learn best in calm, and some in storm. —Willa Cather

How Are You Today?

Jo Ellen Weaver

**"But I trusted in thee, O Lord: I said,
Thou art my God."** —Psalm 31:14

So how are you?" asked my friend Joan the first time I came to church after a miscarriage.

"Oh, just fine," I quickly replied. What I meant was that the bleeding had stopped, my strength was coming back, and my limbs no longer ached all day and night.

I always suppose that is what my kind friends want to know the first few times I see them after having a miscarriage.

Do they really want to know that my heart aches? Do they want to know that I long for the brief pregnancy? That I miss the wee little one who came and left so quickly? How would they react if I'd say that I am grieving, really grieving?

I want to cry out, "Don't worry about me, my physical self. I lost my baby. My baby was snatched away before I ever felt that comforting twitch inside my womb. Am I grieving alone?"

Even my husband and family appear to be more concerned about my health than our loss.

But while I'm crying out to God in the sleepless hours of the morning, He assures me that He sees my aching heart and flowing tears. He reminds me that my friends really do care, but probably have difficulty expressing it because the reality of the baby is not as obvious to them as it is to me. I thank Him that they try to care even when it seems they don't understand.

I arise with one more layer of tissue securely attached to the wound.

> *When a friend loses a loved one, mark your calendar on one month, six months, and one year after that date, so that you can encourage her specifically on those days.*

Love Does Not Envy

Paula Brubaker

> **"Charity suffereth long, and
> is kind; charity envieth not."** —I Corinthians 13:4a

B ut, Lord, were you serious? Charity envies not, even when the pain is generated by miscarriage?"

This turmoil can be so much a part of grieving an infant loss. God knows our debility of heart during the weeks and months that follow disappointment. But how long does He allow us to tolerate unkind feelings toward those prospering and "blooming?"

Jesus feels our human pain. He sees when we gulp and look away to avoid the sister who still carries the promise and date that we lost. He knows whether it is envy or just plain pain. When we can barely interpret our own attitudes, He intercedes for us before the Father.

He gives us a worthwhile reminder in 1 Peter 5. "Knowing that

the SAME afflictions are accomplished in your brethren that are in the world. But the God of all grace… after that you have suffered a while, make you perfect, stablish, strengthen, settle you."

Not only have thousands of other women in the world experienced the same woe I have, but which of the sisters who rejoices today has not previously endured affliction? Yes, their life may presently glow

with heavenly sunbeams, but haven't they also seen their portion of cloudy days? In bygone years has one of them experienced a miscarriage, too? Or her afflictions may be very dissimilar to mine, such as financial difficulty, or unsupportive relatives.

How can I feel envious of her circumstances when God has custom-designed mine? He knows the end from the beginning and will send sadness or joy to each of us in turn, to the end of perfecting, stablishing, strengthening, settling us.

"To him be glory and dominion forever and ever" (1 Peter 5:11). I will ever strive to envy not and to rejoice with the rejoicing… even with tears in my eyes. Amen. ᕤ

Covetous

Martha Snell Nicholson

I used to love this sunny room
With shining windows in a row;
It overlooks my neighbor's yard,
And here I'd sit to write or sew,

But since a certain day last spring
A strange pain burns at my heart's core;
Though I protest I don't know why
I never sit there anymore

Nor write my foolish rhymes; yet deep
Within this aching heart of mine,
I know it is the baby clothes
Which flutter on the neighbor's line.

*Whenever God gives us a cross to bear,
it is a promise that He will also give us strength.*

God of Surprises

Dianna Overholt

"Consider the wondrous works of God." —Job 37:14b

A friend and I have both been surprised recently. I was surprised to have a miscarriage after having two healthy pregnancies. At age 40, she's surprised to be pregnant again. She gave me her maternity dresses after her last one six years ago, and now I'm lending her mine.

I sort through the stack of folded dresses and pull out a favorite apron. Suddenly, tears spring to my eyes. *I'd love to be wearing these dresses, and look down and see a little bulge. I want to feel a kick... a kick that says, "Hi, Mom, I'm growing in here."*

Other things have caught me unexpectedly. Like when a friend told me about a coffee break for the four expectant ladies in the church. I should've been there, sipping coffee and exchanging laughs

and groans about the idiosyncrasies of pregnancy. But I wasn't there. Instead, I'm still trying to get used to the fact that my pregnancy has ended. *There are no more "nine months" to count down.*

Someday I may be surprised with another little bundle, but I know that in my heart it will never be *that one.*

"That one" is probably one of the tiniest and sweetest babies on Jesus' lap right now. I have so many questions for Jesus. Is our baby a boy or a girl? Does he have black hair like the rest of the family? Does Baby know how much we love him?

I suspect the answers are some of the surprises Jesus is keeping for us when we get to heaven.

As hard as it is to say it, I do thank You, Lord, that You are a God of surprises. ✑

Surprise your mother with an unexpected gift.

Afraid to Go

Sue Hooley

**"And the Lord, he it is that doth go before thee;
he will be with thee, he will not fail thee, neither forsake thee:
fear not, neither be dismayed."** —Deuteronomy 31:8

Can you and your family come over tomorrow for lunch?" my friend asked.

"Oh, sure!" I replied. "Thanks for the invitation."

But how can I go? I thought as I hung up the phone. *How can I possibly go to Jason and Lena's?*

I had not held a newborn baby since my miscarriage two months earlier, and Lena had a baby girl. Was I backing myself into a corner? Already I pictured Lena bustling around in her kitchen. The baby would begin to fuss and Lena would look at me and say, "Would you mind holding Krista while I finish dinner preparations?"

How could I do that? Just the sight or sound of a newborn brought tears to my eyes. I tried avoiding such situations. But now I had no choice.

That night I could not go to sleep. My pillow sponged up my tears as once again I relived the emptiness and disappointment of my loss. *God,* I prayed, *I can't even put my thoughts into words, but You know how I feel and You know about tomorrow, too. Please help me!*

> *There is no grief which time does not lessen and soften.* —Cicero

The morning dawned bright and clear. I felt God's strength shining even brighter as our family walked into our friends' home. To my surprise, I even offered to hold the baby.

I'm thankful that I dealt with the pain instead of avoiding it. If we allow ourselves to grieve, healing will come to our hurting hearts.

Miscarriages are difficult. But time heals when God is the Healer. ⤢

Depression?

Marcia Miller

"The eternal God is thy refuge, and underneath are the everlasting arms." —Deuteronomy 33:27a

A few months after we had lost our little one, when everyone expected me to be "okay," I came to the realization that I was NOT okay. What was the matter with me? Why did I feel so dreadfully "blue"? Why didn't I have any energy to work? Why did purpose in life seem so hard to hang onto?

Shocked and ashamed, I eventually recognized these symptoms of depression. I had always thought that depression afflicts those who are not walking closely with the Lord.

Although I experienced only a relatively short period of depression, I gleaned a new compassion for those who fight this deadly foe. It seems to be a common problem after women suffer a

miscarriage and never carry a full-term baby again. Our messed-up hormones trigger the depression.

Once recognized, it's easier to treat. I found some herbal remedies, which helped me to think more clearly. I made a conscious effort to think in constructive patterns. For example, I knew I could not allow the careless comments made out of misunderstanding by others to fester in my soul. I learned that forgiveness is not optional with those who would follow Christ. The little things that bothered me were really quite trivial when seen within the context of the whole picture.

During this difficult time, one verse especially reminded me of the One who upheld me: "The eternal God is thy refuge, and underneath are the everlasting arms" (Deuteronomy 33:27a). Picturing myself in His loving arms comforted me.

Whenever you see the color yellow today,
remind yourself of the sunshine of God's love in your life.

Call Anytime

Marcia Miller

"Call unto me, and I will answer thee, and shew thee great and mighty things, which thou knowest not." —Jeremiah 33:3

Hello, Mom! We arrived safely in Idaho this evening! We had a really great trip. It was so much fun traveling together on a big bus!" I rambled on, answering Mom's questions and enthusiastically recounting the highlights of our trip out West. Catching a glimpse of my watch, I apologized for calling at bedtime. "It's still daylight here, Mom; I didn't realize it was already ten o'clock."

Mom laughed. Then it dawned on me that in Ohio, it was midnight. "Oh, Mom, I forgot about the time change! I am so sorry to wake you up. You were already sleeping, weren't you?"

Evading the question, my dear mother answered with something I'll never forget. "Marcia, I'm so glad you called. I'll sleep much better now, knowing you arrived safely. And I am so glad you had a good trip."

I am 45 years old and have my own family. Yet Mom cared that much about our safety and happiness. It reminded me of another family member. This Father does not sleep at all. He says I can call Him anytime of the day or night. He wants me to tell Him all about my journey. He's concerned about my safety. And amazingly, He cares about me even more than my precious mom does!

Call an old friend and spend some time reminiscing.

Is It Wrong to Grieve?

Marcia Miller

**"And the children of Israel wept for Moses
in the plains of Moab thirty days: so the days of weeping
and mourning for Moses were ended."** —Deuteronomy 34:8

She's just feeling sorry for herself," someone said.

Sorry for herself? I thought incredulously. *My friend is mourning over her miscarriage!*

I also was groping through a maze of grief after losing the baby we were so excited about. Unsure of all the turns and corners in this private maze of mine, the thoughtless statement set me thinking.

Is it wrong to grieve over innocent babies who we know are "in a better place"? Is it selfishness to wish we could cuddle and enjoy them?

While reading through the Old Testament, I discovered some answers. God wanted His people to mourn for their dead. He knew that their emotions couldn't heal if they did not first go through a time of mourning. This thought was very comforting to me. I had felt that it was expected of me to just go on with life as normal, as soon as I'd regained my strength. But my Lord knew that this was not as easy as it sounded. He knew that there would be days when I would need to cry. He understood.

But there was also something else in the Old Testament stories. After a specified time, the Israelites were to come out of mourning and go on with their regular routines. This too, spoke to me. The Lord knew that I would become sick mentally if I grieved too long. He did not want my sadness to deteriorate into self-pity or bitterness. It would be wrong for me to feel bitterness towards a friend when I hold her newborn baby. But it is not wrong when tears pool as I cuddle her precious one to myself and wonder how my little one would have looked.

It helped to know that the Lord made my fragile emotions. He wants me to care deeply. He understands when I hurt. And He will help me to become a more caring person because I have known grief. ✎

Compile a memory scrapbook of your miscarried child.
Include cards you've received, words of
encouragement, pressed flowers, and verses from
Scripture that are precious to you.

And Joseph fell upon his father's face, and wept upon him, and kissed him.

And Joseph commanded his servants the physicians to embalm his father: and the physicians embalmed Israel.

And forty days were fulfilled for him; for so are fulfilled the days of those which are embalmed: and the Egyptians mourned for him threescore and ten days.

And when the days of his mourning were past, Joseph spake unto the house of Pharaoh, saying, If now I have found grace in your eyes, speak, I pray you, in the ears of Pharaoh, saying,

My father made me swear, saying, Lo, I die: in my grave which I have digged for me in the land of Canaan, there shalt thou bury me. Now therefore let me go up, I pray thee, and bury my father, and I will come again.

And Pharaoh said, Go up, and bury thy father, according as he made thee swear.

And Joseph went up to bury his father: and with him went up all the servants of Pharaoh, the elders of his house, and all the elders of the land of Egypt,

And all the house of Joseph, and his brethren, and his father's house: only their little ones, and their flocks, and their herds, they left in the land of Goshen.

Genesis 50:1–8

Sing Before the Throne

Dianna Overholt

"The Lord is my strength and my shield;… with my song will I praise him." —Psalm 28:7

What would you think if you knew that someone sang before an audience just hours after having a miscarriage?

That's what my sister's mother-in-law did.

Jim and Ruth Ann had been married for seven years before she finally conceived. Six weeks into her pregnancy, they went away on a chorus tour. It was while she was getting ready for the last program of the trip that she discovered she was bleeding. And cramping. Before long she knew her pregnancy was over.

She didn't tell anyone but Jim. The evening service was about to begin. A little white in the face, she took her place with the others. And she sang a solo.

She wasn't calloused. In fact, she felt completely opposite of that. But in her shock and numbness, she turned to the one thing she loved doing the most—singing to her Father.

Have you tried singing yet?

When you are tired of thinking about all the *I-should'ves,* the *what-ifs,* and the *whys,* think about singing.

When you have exhausted your tissue supply again but the tears just won't stop, reach for a song.

Pick up a songbook or think of a favorite hymn. You don't even have to sing aloud. You can sing in your mind. The important thing is to lift your devotion to the One who loves you the most.

Think of it, your little one is with a choir of millions. Perhaps even singing a solo. ✎

When you get dressed in the morning,
put on the "garment of praise." When discouragement or doubt
threatens, remember your garment. If the song
"Garment of Praise" helps, go ahead, sing it!

Garment of Praise

David Ingles

Chorus:
Put on the garment of praise for the spirit of heaviness,
Lift up your voice to God;
Praise with the Spirit and with understanding,
Oh, magnify the Lord!

All you that mourn in Zion,
I have authority;
To appoint unto you in Zion,
Oil of joy that will set you free.

Lift up the hands that hang down,
Lift up the voice now still;
Give unto God continuous praise,
Sing forth from Zion's hill.

Sing to Yahweh, alleluia!
Worship and praise our God;
Praise and adore Him, bow down before Him,
Oh, magnify the Lord!

At the Other End

Sue Hooley

"There is a friend that sticketh closer than a brother." —Proverbs 18:24b

The knot in Eric's stomach tightened with each curve on his way home from work. *What kind of mood will Karla be in tonight?* he wondered. *The fact that she was smiling this morning does not mean she will be smiling now.* Karla had been on a seesaw of emotions ever since her miscarriage two months earlier. *I am sad, too, but somehow I don't feel the pain like she does.*

"Hi honey, I'm home!" Eric said, stepping inside. "How was your day?"

"It was okay, I guess. I felt so tired and… and lonely, too."

"Did you take a nap?" Eric questioned.

"Oh, no!" Karla answered shortly. "I would never get all of my work done if I took a nap."

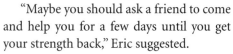

"Maybe you should ask a friend to come and help you for a few days until you get your strength back," Eric suggested.

"I couldn't stand having someone around all day. I'll make out just fine. I don't think you understand how I feel," she finished as the tears began to spill down her cheeks.

Eric was quiet. *She is tired but she doesn't want to take a nap. Her work is not getting done, yet she doesn't want help. She is lonely, but she doesn't want anyone around. I just don't know what else to offer,* he thought helplessly.

"You are right, honey, I don't understand how you feel," Eric said gently as he slipped his arm around his sobbing wife. "But I do love you and we will get through this together."

Tell your husband that you love him. He's that
special someone hanging on at the other end of the seesaw
and he may be getting more of a ride than he bargained for!
Remember that your balance directly affects him.

He's Still Working on Me

Rosey Miller

"The Lord will perfect that which concerneth me." —Psalm 138:8a

The Lord will perfect that which concerneth me." Was God really doing that? Could I believe this promise even on a gray winter day when I so badly wanted to be holding a warm little baby? But instead, my hands were sewing a dolly for my daughter.

Snip, snip. My scissors rounded the doll's pattern pieces. Suddenly I thought of how God is still patiently forming me. I have a lot of edges that need rounding. Is that why He has put multiple miscarriages into the pattern of my life?

I started sewing the separate pieces of cloth together and they began forming a doll. God reminded me that He is fitting together the pieces of my life according to the finished product He wants to see. I do not know what the final object will be, but I need to follow His instructions.

Spend the evening reading to your family.

We filled the doll with rice and stuffing to give it a floppy, flexible feeling, more cuddly than a plastic doll. Flexibility? Another quality He is teaching me, to bend and be shaped at His will.

Last of all I embroidered the face and hair. What a good reminder that God knows how many hairs I have on my head. He cares for me!

But the lines on my face are still being formed. If my heart holds bitterness because things haven't gone as I'd like, it will show on my face. I filled in the curve of the tiny pink mouth and prayed that my final expression will tell a story of peace with God.

Is God perfecting that which concerns me? He certainly is.

Three Important Words

Dianna Overholt

"It is a good thing to give thanks unto the Lord, and to sing praises unto thy name, O most High." —Psalm 92:1

These three words were uttered in the belly of a whale.

Daniel spoke them just before he faced a king who had ordered his murder.

Jesus prayed them as He held seven loaves and a few fishes, the entire buffet for a multitude.

In the most impossible of circumstances, these men exemplified the words that would later be given as our standard. What were the words?

Thank you, God. They gave thanks! Look what happened after they voiced their gratitude.

The whale suddenly felt the urge to get rid of its churning baggage.

The king retracted his execution decree. Four thousand people dined on the loaves and fishes. Thankfulness was an ingredient that God used to change these hopeless circumstances.

Can we give thanks for the situations in which we find ourselves? (Even if we are wearing the garment of heaviness?) I thought about all of this as my son was putting on pajamas and finding his little stuffed kitty. As he knelt by his pillow, this is what he prayed:

"Dear Jesus, thank You for all this wonderful world. Thank You for all the little creatures that live here. Thank you that Mommy got me Zebra Cakes to eat; thank you that Mommy got me a new toothbrush. Amen."

I listened with an open heart, realizing that he was a step ahead of me in understanding thankfulness. He didn't pray about what he does not have; instead he thanked the Lord for what he does have. Little things like Zebra Cakes!

Thankfulness is all about my whole attitude. Although I may not be ready to utter, "Thank you, God," immediately after a loss in my life, God knows that I am thankful for Him, and He sees the desires of my heart.

When I can sincerely say the three important words, *Thank You, God,* He can begin a marvelous work in my life. ✎

I can no other answer ever make but
thanks... and ever thanks. —William Shakespeare

Now when Daniel knew that the writing was signed, he went into his house; and his windows being open in his chamber toward Jerusalem, he kneeled upon his knees three times a day, and prayed, and gave thanks before his God, as he did aforetime.

Daniel 6:10

Rocking Friends' Little Babies

Marcia Miller

"He healeth the broken in heart, and bindeth up their wounds." —Psalm 147:3

"Oh, Mommy, we wanted that baby so much!" my little girl wailed, trying to absorb the disappointment of my second miscarriage. I felt so utterly unable to assuage her grief. (If only there were a box of Band-Aids for this!) Wrapping my arms about her, I wept with her.

"We'll have to take every opportunity we can to care for others' children, okay?" I suggested to my girls standing near me. "That may help to heal our hurt."

It *was* healing. In the years that followed, we found many

opportunities. There were two families to whom we grew especially close. My girls snapped pictures, braided little pigtails, read their favorite children's stories, and rocked babies to sleep. We loved holding a little cousin who would have almost been a twin to one we lost, and taking pictures of her.

We learned together to smile again. God was good. His promise that He will heal the brokenhearted was meant for us.

Take some good snapshots of your friend's children.
Make copies and give them to your friend.

Identifying with Elijah

Annette Bechtel

"…and after the fire, a still small voice." —I Kings 19:12b

It had been a difficult year. I could identify perfectly with Elijah.

Just days after I miscarried a tiny son, my mom was diagnosed with terminal lung cancer. She lived for only three more months. A week after her death, my brother's wife miscarried their first child. A few months later, my twin sister lost their baby during her first trimester.

It is enough now, O Lord! I cried out with Elijah. I wanted to give vent to ugly thoughts churning in my mind. *What next, Lord? Why pick on our family while so many others sail through life with no ripples? Do You really care?*

I'm grateful that God doesn't look the other way when grief grabs us and we question His moves. He doesn't leave us desolate when despair sends us searching for Elijah's juniper.

Instead, He urges us to get up and eat the angel food of His Word for nourishment. He pleads with us to learn who He really is—the God of all comfort. He asks us to tend to the responsibilities of family life and reminds us that a host of friends supports us.

> *Often the test of courage is not to die but to live.*
>
> —Alfieri

He did that for me.

In time, I could thank Him for the earthquake, the wind, and the fire; for through such trials comes the greatest capacity for receiving His still small voice of comfort. ✑

Sisters

Dianna Overholt

**"And above all these things put on charity,
which is the bond of perfectness."** —Colossians 3:14

I have just received a special note in the mail from my sister. Not from my youngest sister (the one with whom I rarely argue!), but from the sister who has been my opposite from the day she was born 21 months after me. If I wanted the light off in our room, she wanted it on. If I wanted to relax at my desk, she preferred pounding a volleyball. How we made life interesting for each other! And so I read…

> …*Thank you again for the bouquet of flowers!*
> *I wish I would have done something for you when you had your miscarriage. I had no idea what a miscarriage was like. Now, unfortunately, I do.*
> *It seems that we've both started our families in heaven already. That's one of the most comforting thoughts for me.*

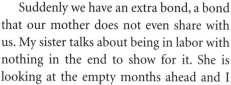

Suddenly we have an extra bond, a bond that our mother does not even share with us. My sister talks about being in labor with nothing in the end to show for it. She is looking at the empty months ahead and I sympathize, because I know.

Have the first cousins, our children, found each other in heaven? I like to think that they have. They are one more link in the bond that makes us more than sisters by birth.

I also feel a new empathy with my sisters in Christ. An older sister comes to share tears and hugs. She has not forgotten losing her little one almost 30 years ago. It has been nine years for another sister, but fragile memories are still tucked away in her mother-heart…

What can I do to strengthen this bond with my sisters?

I want to give a Mother's Day card to the sister whose firstborn is in heaven. I want to put my arms around the expectant mother whose latest pregnancy ended in a miscarriage, and tell her I am praying for her. I want to be considerate and careful in the things that I say to my sisters. I want to remember that hurts and pains can run very deep.

Our heavenly Father can use our shared experiences to enrich us, better us, and make us more than sisters by birth. ⇌

Bake some sweet rolls or prepare a casserole
for a friend who is going through a difficult time.

> *Charity suffereth long, and is kind; charity envieth not; charity vaunteth not itself, is not puffed up,*
> *Doth not behave itself unseemly, seeketh not her own, is not easily provoked, thinketh no evil;*
> *Rejoiceth not in iniquity, but rejoiceth in the truth;*
> *Beareth all things, believeth all things, hopeth all things, endureth all things.*
> *Charity never faileth...*
> *And now abideth faith, hope, charity, these three; but the greatest of these is charity.*
>
> I Corinthians 13:4–8a, 13

The Field of My Heart

Paula Brubaker

**"The sacrifices of God are a broken spirit:
a broken and a contrite heart, O God,
thou wilt not despise."** —Psalm 51:17

I have just spent a relaxing evening alongside my husband in the tractor cab, watching him disk the rich, dark soil. The clods tumble over each other as the blade passes through them and I marvel at his persistence.

For even though the whole field has been covered, he starts the process over again. Yes, I do see the difference it makes; the soul becomes finer and the lumps of earth smaller. By now I presume he will be satisfied and proceed to the adjoining field. After all, we are in the middle of spring rush and acres await him!

But no, he says that this field will need a third pass. And so I  patiently watch as the dust rolls and the fine soil becomes finer yet.

The analogy of it all became clearer in my mind as I listened to a Sunday morning devotional about a broken heart. My heart had felt so broken lately and I hung onto every word. A broken heart is one God can bless, one God can use (Psalm 51:17) and one that He is near to (Psalm 34:18). Our hearts cannot be broken without sorrow (Proverbs 15:13). And yes, it is a heart that He can bind up and heal (Psalm 147:3, Luke 4:18).

The speaker used the example of the soil the plowman works. It takes pass after pass to break it and to make it the kind of soil that will yield abundantly.

Inwardly I ponder, *Is this why my heart has been broken and cut to shreds for the third time this year? Before every miscarriage our hopes have soared, our tears have passed, and we are truly convinced that at last our Father has chosen to give us our share of blessing for patience and pain. But lo, we suddenly realize He isn't finished yet! The cruel blade cuts across our hearts of flesh once more. And we cry out in pain,*

"Why again, dear Lord?"

But our God knows what He is doing! He makes the soil finer so that we will bring forth much more precious fruit to His glory.

Take my heart, oh Father, and plow it again if that should seem good in Thy sight. ❧

The plant cut down to the root does not hate.
It uses all its strength to grow once more.

—Elizabeth Jane Coatsworth

Doth the plowman plow all day to sow? Doth he open and break the clods of his ground?

When he hath made plain the face thereof, doth he not cast abroad the fitches, and scatter the cummin, and cast in the principal wheat and the appointed barley and the rie in their place?

For his God doth instruct him to discretion, and doth teach him.

For the fitches are not threshed with a threshing instrument, neither is a cart wheel turned about upon the cummin; but the fitches are beaten out with a staff, and the cummin with a rod.

Bread corn is bruised; because he will not ever be threshing it, nor break it with the wheel of his cart, nor bruise it with his horsemen.

This also cometh forth from the Lord of hosts, which is wonderful in counsel, and excellent in working.

Isaiah 28:24–29

Family Album

Marcia Miller

"A woman that feareth the Lord, she shall be praised." —Proverbs 31:30b

Memories.

Opening the scrapbook of my mind, I page through pictures of the past. I smile at the one of my youngest cuddled in my arms as we eagerly read a new copy of *The Biggest Bear*. Here's one of us counting a pen full of squealing piglets. I flip another page and see our family on a sweaty June morning, singing as we clean big buckets of green beans. Later, on winter evenings, we're gathered around the table munching on warm, buttery popcorn.

I treasure these memories of our children's growing-up days.

But what will they remember?

I'm convinced that we make memories with our children not only

by taking them to the zoo, or reading them their favorite books, but by the everyday life we live. Happy memories are created by working with them, answering their questions, listening to their stories. But we are also making memories with them when we are harsh or hard to please. Especially when we are overly tired or feeling blue and physically low, we have the potential to create hurtful memories.

How will they remember me dealing with crises in my life? My reactions to loss and disappointment are also making memories with them. When they face their own losses, I hope they will be able to look back and reflect, *"Now I understand how Mom felt. It must have been difficult for her, but I know she relied on the Lord."*

I hope my children are pasting this kind of memory in the scrapbooks of their minds. ✎

No man is poor who has had a godly mother.

—Abraham Lincoln

My Priceless Husband

Marcia Miller

"Many waters cannot quench love."

—Song of Solomon 8:7a

As I turned to receive my husband's *I'm-so-glad-to-be-home* hug, he whispered, "I brought a little something to remind you that I love you. It's in my lunch pail." Gaily I opened the not-quite-empty Coleman. Inside I found my favorite kind of candy bar. "Thanks, my love!" The light is back in my eyes.

It seems my husband has a sixth sense, or maybe I am just very easy to read! He has boosted my morale so often when I am feeling blue.

I don't want to take for granted the dedicated man who has stood behind and with me through the trauma of miscarriage and recovery. Although husbands don't have the hormonal stresses we do, they do have to exercise patience with an unpredictable wife. (I won't argue as to which is worse!) So I want to do my best to show my husband how much I appreciate his support as he wrestles with his own pain.

List five things (or more!) that you appreciate about your husband. Give him the list.

I trusted my husband with my worst struggles and hurdles during the difficult months and years that followed. I knew he would still keep faith in me. He knew me inside out. I never realized before how much it meant to have someone who believed in me, even when I couldn't understand myself.

I thank the Lord for His goodness in giving me a patient husband, my blessing in the valleys of life.

Lulled By Thy Light

Dianna Overholt

"As one whom his mother comforteth, so will I comfort you." —Isaiah 66:13a

Sunday morning, December 22.

The worship service was just beginning, the first song announced.

I squeezed my daughter closer to me on my lap. My heart was so full, I was afraid I would disgrace myself (again!) by letting my emotions spill out. Perhaps if I held Angela close and smelled her hair…

A year ago today a friend lost her baby. She had been dreading today. *How is she doing?* I wondered.

Ahead of me, two ladies' well-rounded tummies attested to the closeness of their due dates. *I shouldn't have a lap, either,* I whispered

into Angela's hair. *My due date was supposed to be soon, too. I dread the day when these ladies have their babies.*

The song leader had chosen Star of the East. Suddenly I heard the words of the song in a way I never had before.

> Star of the East, O Bethlehem Star,
> Guiding us on to heaven afar;
> Sorrow and grief are lulled by thy light,
> Thou hope of each mortal in death's
>   lonely night.

Sorrow and grief are lulled… by Thy light.

Jesus, thank You.

You do not remove our sorrows or our grief. But oh, when we come to You, You lull them. You carry them and rock them to sleep for a while.

Sometimes they awaken soon, but the lull is always a sweet resting in You.

Star of the East, undimmed by each cloud,
What if the storms of grief gather loud?
Faithful and pure thy rays beam to save,
Still bright o'er the cradle and bright o'er the grave.

Sweet Bethlehem Star, I feel the warmth of Your light and I come to worship You. ⌒

Light a candle.

It is of the Lord's mercies that we are not consumed, because his compassions fail not.

They are new every morning: great is thy faithfulness.

The Lord is my portion, saith my soul; therefore will I hope in him.

The Lord is good unto them that wait for him, to the soul that seeketh him.

It is good that a man should both hope and quietly wait for the salvation of the Lord.

Lamentations 3:22–26

He's the Same

Dianna Overholt

**"But thou art the same, and
thy years shall have no end."** —Psalm 102:27

Today is tougher than I thought it would be.

My due date is only three days away. The baby that should be almost here has been gone for six months. I am trying not to remember that my first two children were born three days early. But I'm fixing supper for a friend who just had a baby, and it's hard not to think about it.

Her baby's round little face is adorable. He twists his mouth several times in that yawn that only a newborn can make. Her house shines from a doting aunt's scrubbing, but when I return to mine I am faced with toys, strewn clothes, and a mountain of dishes, not to mention the smell of fresh turkey manure from a neighboring field.

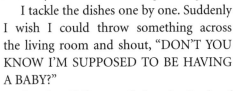

I tackle the dishes one by one. Suddenly I wish I could throw something across the living room and shout, "DON'T YOU KNOW I'M SUPPOSED TO BE HAVING A BABY?"

So what if I'm not facing the Battle of the Bulge in the months ahead. Right now I wouldn't care if I looked as big as a... a hippopotamus.

So what if our house is so small that it would be hard to find room for another crib. I would be glad to cut a hole in the bedroom wall and stick one in there.

Sigh.

I know how I should be feeling and all the proper things I should be thinking.

And soon I will think on them. This frustrating moment will pass. It starts to recede even now as I pause before the verse on our wall and say, "Thank You, Jesus. You are the same. *You are the SAME!* Yesterday, today, and forever."

*Remember the more chaotic the situation,
the calmer you need to be.* —H. Jackson Brown, Jr., 2002

New Memories

Sue Hooley

**"Ointment and perfume rejoice the heart:
so doth the sweetness of a man's friend
by hearty counsel."** —Proverbs 27:9

A re you busy with Christmas baking?" my sister asked.
"Not really," I replied. "I just don't feel like doing much this year."

"Why not?" she inquired. "You usually do a lot."

I sucked in my breath. Did I dare admit the truth? "Well," I began, "I just feel like ignoring Christmas. Last year I was all involved in making cookies and candies, then I miscarried and it took the light out of everything. Christmas carols, Christmas cookies, Christmas plans—they all bring back memories of losing my baby last year and it's a depressing feeling."

"I understand that this is a trying time," she sympathized. "But maybe you need to make some new memories. Make a new kind of cookies with your children. Do some special things with them so that when you look back at this Christmas, you will have good memories. If nothing else, do it for the sake of your children."

Make good memories… For the sake of your children… The words went around in my mind. *Can I come out of my comfort zone and make cookies, sing Christmas carols, and light some candles?*

*Yesterday is gone.
Tomorrow is not yet come.
We have only today.
Let us begin.*
—Mother Teresa

The children will enjoy making these cutout cookies, I thought as I thumbed through my favorite recipes. *I will mix up a batch and tonight we can bake and decorate them.*

Later, as we sat in candlelight sipping hot cocoa and eating lop-headed snowmen, I was rewarded with the children's laughter and their enjoyment of this special evening. I suddenly realized that doing it for the sake of the children was really for the sake of myself! ✎

Journal Entry on Due Date

Danette Martin

**"This is the day which the Lord hath made;
we will rejoice and be glad in it."** —Psalm 118:24

Randy's due date today. I'm grieving double: over what was and over what could've been. (Is that the measure of grief for all deaths, varying according to the age of the one who died and the griever's relationship to the one gone?)

I reflect over the goodness of God in the past months. Where would I be if God hadn't allowed afflictions to touch my life? I think I'd be a stressed-out workaholic, doing things on my own strength and believing I'm capable of running the show! *Oh God, thank You for delivering me from such a life... keep teaching me... I need You more than ever.*

I want to major on two things today—focus on God's goodness to me, and do something for persons who are grieving or hurting in some way, too.

Signs of God's goodness:

- ⚘ a brilliant sunrise on my morning walk
- ⚘ gorgeous spring bouquet from m'dear who "loves me as we miss Randy together"
- ⚘ we don't need to buy a new fridge; the problem was only a clogged drain (a blueberry stuck in there!) and a freezer control set too high
- ⚘ cards from my sis and sister-in-law; a care-box (with a package for each of us to open) in the mail from my brother's family
- ⚘ all-over beautiful, warm day (We visited Randy's plot at the cemetery on our way to pick up schoolchildren. The girls skipped about on the grass and chattered happily in the midst of all those death-signs. How could I be morbid?)
- ⚘ meaningful song: we sang "All the Way My Saviour Leads Me" at prayer meeting tonight; hug and comforting talk from a grandma at church

You know, dreading this day was much worse than actually living it. *Thank You, God, for ample evidence of Your goodness!* 〜

---

*Every day, stop before something beautiful long enough
to say, "Isn't that b-e-a-u-t-i-f-u-l!"* —Palmer

This is the day which the Lord hath made; we will rejoice and be glad in it.

Save now, I beseech thee, O Lord: O Lord, I beseech thee, send now prosperity.

Blessed be he that cometh in the name of the Lord: we have blessed you out of the house of the Lord.

God is the Lord, which hath shewed us light: bind the sacrifice with cords, even unto the horns of the altar.

Thou art my God, and I will praise thee: thou art my God, I will exalt thee.

O give thanks unto the Lord; for he is good: for his mercy endureth for ever.

Psalm 118:24–29

Snowdrops

Danette Martin

"For God, who commanded the light to shine out of darkness, hath shined in our hearts, to give the light of the knowledge of the glory of God in the face of Jesus Christ." —II Corinthians 4:6

It's November. I lie on white sheets with the hospital phone to my ear. My mother-in-law is saying, "I'll always remember where I was when I got the call about your baby. I was out planting bulbs. Would there be space in your flower bed where I could plant some extras? Then in April, when your baby would've been due, you can enjoy the spring flowers...."

My voice thick with tears, I manage to thank her and make suggestions for a planting location. People have been just too thoughtful, my dear mom-in-law included.

It's April. Signs of spring have been only teasers. Winter's grasp releases one icy finger at a time. "Come on, snow," I mentally urge, "Leave! There are globes of hope under you ready to boost new growth."

The tiniest bulbs can't wait. Fragile hoop skirt petals surpass the drifts in height and whiteness. Snowdrops. Such brave beauty.

It should be April in my life, too. I implore the winter of loss to hasten its departure, but circumstances keep dumping more snow. A tooth filling breaks, fear and I do battle as I prepare to share a testimony in public, heart palpitations call for medical testing, and tension mounts in the midst of church problems. Can I manifest Christ in me by pushing life upward through banks of trouble and perplexity?

Every April, the snowdrops will remind me, encourage me, and fill me with hope. ✑

Plant a flowering tree in memory of your baby.

Following

Marilyn Miller

"My soul followeth hard after thee:
thy right hand upholdeth me." —Psalm 63:8

My attention was fixed on the group of preschoolers reciting their Sunday school verse at the front of the church. Two of our own healthy, robust sons were among the children gathered up there. But the child that caught my eye was not mine, but another mother's child, and in my mind I was comparing him with the one we didn't have.

Jason's mother had been expecting just a few weeks earlier than the due date the doctor had given me. We had so much fun comparing notes. Then suddenly, I was out of the nine-month race. I couldn't help but follow in my heart where our child would be now. What might have been if things had turned out differently for us?

Later that afternoon when the children were occupied elsewhere, I mentioned my melancholy musings to my husband. "I know," he replied sympathetically. "But if we had kept that one, we wouldn't have this one."

Watch the sun set.

My eyes followed the direction he indicated with his head and came to rest on one of the boys. Caring, considerate of others, steady, dependable, and mischievous—a carbon copy of his daddy! Would I trade? No, of course not!

Our hearts will always keep a place for our missing child. And I know I will always follow him in my mind by watching other children who are as old as he would be. But God, who knows all things, sees the future as we cannot, and in His infinite wisdom and understanding makes no mistakes. Resting in Him gives me peace.

Matter-of-Fact Happiness

Sue Hooley

"My times are in thy hand." —Psalm 31:15a

In just a few minutes I will know if my suspicions are true. My hands shake and my throat feels dry as I hover over the pregnancy test and wait for results. And then-n-n... Positive! Wow! I am shocked, amazed, and tickled pink!

I go directly to dreamland. Is it a boy or a girl? Where will we set the crib? I can't wait to tell my daughter. Who will be our maid?

My dream abruptly ends and my heart fills with dread. What if I miscarry? My latest two pregnancies ended in miscarriages; what if this one does, too? Grabbing my dreams, I tuck them into a corner of my heart. *Stay there until I hear a heartbeat.*

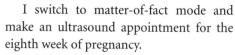

I switch to matter-of-fact mode and make an ultrasound appointment for the eighth week of pregnancy.

Sometimes I feel nauseated and my hopes rise. Other times I feel crampy and wonder if life has already fled. I try to pray, but I'm not sure what to ask for, so I plead for grace to go through this uncertain time.

Only three more days until I know the truth! Time, go fast. I want to hear that heartbeat! Slow down, time. I'm afraid I'll hear silence.

Little one, are you up in heaven or are you under my heart? I want to love you lots, but I'm afraid to love too much.

Only three more days...

O aching time! O moments big as years!

—John Keats

Be of Good Courage

Annette Bechtel

> "Wait on the Lord: be of good courage,
> and he shall strengthen thine heart: wait, I say,
> on the Lord." —Psalm 27:14

Being pregnant again after miscarrying was like being in the middle of a swinging bridge. The closer I got to the 17th week, the "fatal date," the more I felt like the bridge was swaying. I couldn't turn around and retrace my steps; I was petrified to walk ahead into the looming fog of what-ifs. Even my white-knuckled grip on the handropes did little to secure a clutch of control on my life.

Those forty weeks were a lengthy lesson on trust. I often needed David's message in Psalm 27:14, "Wait on the Lord: be of good courage, and he shall strengthen thine heart: wait, I say, on the Lord."

It took courage to lift up my head when I felt drained of physical and emotional energy. It took patience to cheerfully wait for the due date. It took constant commitment to relax in God's plan for this baby's life—or death.

Read the book
Keep A Quiet Heart
by Elizabeth Elliot.

There were many reminders of the Lord's leading and numerous refuelings of His strength during those weeks. But when I joyfully, triumphantly held our healthy newborn, I realized in a greater dimension how very gently and lovingly I had been cradled in His hands every step of the way. ⌒

There Will Your Heart Be Also

Paula Brubaker

**"Set your affection on things above,
not on things on the earth."** —Colossians 3:2

Something as simple as framing a photograph of one's children can be a bittersweet moment.

The picture that I slid into a frame was missing three faces—the faces of our children that we've never seen. The two smiling back at me had become so precious. I didn't hesitate to write the caption "Our Little Treasures" above the picture and underneath I added the verse "Every good gift and every perfect gift is from above."

Our little treasures. The words were repeated the next Sunday morning when our minister chose his sermon text from Matthew 6. He applied laying up treasures to raising our family in such a way that they will be in heaven at the end of life. Treasures being the children.

Why, this is exactly what we were doing! They now numbered three that we had laid up in heaven, and what caught my notice was the next verse—"For where your treasure is, there will your heart be also."

Hadn't my husband and I been more mindful of heaven since our latest loss? Hadn't the longing been greater since our disappointment, to leave this pain and heartache and these tears forever behind?

Truly, our "laying up treasures in heaven" had that very effect on us. We wonder what each little treasure looks like, up in that heavenly city. Will we be able to hold them when we arrive? Are they bringing pleasure to our heavenly Father and the saints of all the ages?

Our little ones in heaven are our treasures; there they cannot be corrupted or stolen. And there our hearts are also! ✎

Make a charitable contribution in memory of your baby.

Father's Day

Dianna Overholt

**"The Lord shall be thine everlasting light,
and the days of thy mourning shall be ended."** —Isaiah 60:20b

I love Father's Day. It is refreshingly familiar, just as my father is. I grin as I watch him go through his traditional shake-the-gift, guess-what-it-is routine. He holds up the wrapped one that I've given him, positive that it contains chocolates. I smile smugly. (He'll be guessing a while before he thinks of Scottish shortbread!)

A few hours later we are ready to go visit Grandpa. Only this time we're not going to the old farmhouse. Instead, we will be at a gravesite dug only three months ago. Grandpa's grave. My father's father.

It's the first time I can remember that Dad is not carrying a Father's Day card. Instead, he appears from the garden with a small bouquet that he's picked. Orange poppies. Pink roses. Yellow daisies. Purple strawflowers. A man's bouquet. He doesn't say anything as he looks at the blossoms, but his hand is trembling.

I want to throw my arms around him and cry and cry. I've picked "good-bye" bouquets, too. Bouquets in my mind of baby's breath and pale pink rosebuds for a grave we don't have.

Even so, come, Lord Jesus.
—Apostle John

Does one ever get done saying good-bye? How do you say good-bye to someone who has been bone-of-your-bone, flesh-of-your-flesh, and heart-of-your-heart, whether it has been for 50 years or for only a few months?

I think I know now why there are so many flower-touched graves.

But we aren't the only ones giving bouquets. For every flower we've ever placed, we receive bunches from our Father in return. Forget-me-nots straight from heaven wrapped in the verse, "I will never leave thee, nor forsake thee." Long-stemmed red roses with the tag, "I have loved thee with an everlasting love." Delicate white snowdrops saying, "I am... the bright and morning star."

His deeply-rooted promises are centerpieces from heaven, freshly delivered to us. If you lean close enough you can catch their fragrant undertones—*I have your loved one with Me. I will return for you. Keep watching…*

Did you catch that? The real *Father's Day* is yet to come!

I can't wait. Although I may never figure out how to say "Good-bye," I KNOW how I am going to say "Hello!" ⬡

Violence shall no more be heard in thy land, wasting nor destruction within thy borders; but thou shalt call thy walls Salvation, and thy gates Praise.

The sun shall be no more thy light by day; neither for brightness shall the moon give light unto thee: but the Lord shall be unto thee an everlasting light, and thy God thy glory.

Thy sun shall no more go down; neither shall thy moon withdraw itself: for the Lord shall be thine everlasting light, and the days of thy mourning shall be ended.

Thy people also shall be all righteous: they shall inherit the land for ever, the branch of my planting, the work of my hands, that I may be glorified.

Isaiah 60:18–21